Samuel Ryder

The Man Behind The Ryder Cup

Samuel Ryder

Samuel Ryder

The Man Behind The Ryder Cup

The Biography of Samuel Ryder

by Peter Fry

Foreword by
Bernard Gallacher

Wright Press, Dorset 2010

ISBN 978-0-9539087-1-4

Designed and typeset in 11/14pt. Caslon by
Hughes & Company
Kempsey, Worcestershire, England

Printed by Henry Ling Limited
The Dorset Press, Dorchester

Published by
Wright Press, 30 Holzwickede Court,
Weymouth, Dorset DT3 6FG

Samuel Ryder

The Man Behind The Ryder Cup

Peter Fry

*This book is dedicated to
my mother (Jessie) and my father (Donald)
for their love and understanding which
made this publication possible*

Contents

Acknowledgements   ix

Foreword   xi

Introduction   xiii

1   Early Years   1

2   Samuel the Seedsman   12

3   Religious Foundation   32

4   Civic Duties   43

5   The Marlborough House Years   55

6   Addicted to Golf   66

7   Heath and Heather Sponsorship   76

8   Initiating The Ryder Cup   95

9   Golf Sponsor Extraordinary   117

10 Goodbye and Thanks   135

Bibliography   145

Acknowledgements

FOR MUCH of the family history I am greatly indebted to various relations of the Ryder family. In particular I have to thank Samuel Ryder's grand-daughter Mary Moore for permission to use material taken from her mother's little-known but quite splendid booklets. Similarly, I thank Yvonne Larg for letting me use information contained in the booklet written by her father Tom Anderson-Davis who drew up the deed of trust for the Ryder Cup. Additionally, John Ryder-Smith and Gwyneth Mackenzie have also greatly assisted the project with photographs or information.

In keeping with Samuel Ryder's many interests, a variety of historical sources also needed to be contacted. Accordingly I am most grateful to the following, whether for information or photographs, or, in some cases, both:-

Mary Davies; Colin Lawless; John Oldfield; Andrew Trevett; Sotheby's of London; Trafford Local Studies Centre, Sale; South Warwickshire Stratford Library, Stratford-on-Avon; Loreto College, St. Albans; Independent Chapel, St. Albans; Trinity United Reform Church, St. Albans; St. Albans Museums; St. Albans Central Library; Hertfordshire Archives and Local Studies, Hertford; The British Newspaper Library, Colindale; The General Register Office, Southport; The Lindley Library, The Royal Horticultural Society, London; Royal Botanic Gardens, Kew; The Michael Hobbs Collection; The Trustees of the Ryder Estate; The Professional Golfers' Association; Stratford-on-Avon Golf Club and The Hulton Getty Picture Collection, London.

I very much thank Samuel Ryder's home golf club – Verulam Golf Club – for permission to use their copyright photographs of F. O. Salisbury's portrait of Samuel Ryder in mayoral robes and Samuel Ryder holding the Ryder Cup on the Clubhouse verandah. Should any reader wish to know more about Samuel Ryder, I can recommend for further reading Samuel Ryder (1858-1936) by Wm. B. Murgatroyd and A. A. Booth.

I also appreciate the many hours of proofreading undertaken by my good friend Keith Stott. Finally, my special thanks must go to Bernard Gallacher for contributing the foreword to this book. As both player and captain, he has enjoyed a distinguished Ryder Cup career and understands the pressures and excitement that makes the Ryder Cup the greatest team event in golf.

P. F.

Foreword

ONE BIG advance in professional golf over the years has been the status of the club professionals. At the beginning of the twentieth century they were not permitted to set foot inside the clubhouse of a golf club. The gentry who controlled the clubs looked upon the shabbily-dressed professional as merely a servant of the club whose place was confined to the professional's shop.

There is no doubt that the famous players Henry Cotton and Walter Hagen did much to improve the lot of the professional golfer. However probably the biggest change amongst peoples' attitudes came about courtesy of Samuel Ryder. He was saddened by the lowly status of the club professionals and decided to champion their cause.

This well-researched book illustrates the amazing number of tournaments and challenge matches that made Samuel Ryder the greatest sponsor of British professional golf in the 1920s. At the time there were few professional tournaments for sponsorship was a rarity and recession became a way of life.

Ryder's generous sponsorship of Abe Mitchell failed to realize his dream of seeing Mitchell win the Open Championship. However his subsequent act of donating the Ryder Cup has had a far greater impact and it is interesting to read of Ryder's precise contribution to the early years of the contest.

Ryder could hardly have foreseen the profound long term effect this event would have on the world of golf. The excitement generated by the Ryder Cup has seen the event develop into a massive commercial operation. In turn, this has fuelled enormous interest in golf in general, leading to increased levels of sponsorship and prize money. A further benefit allows for some of the event's profits to be put back into assisting the grass roots of the game.

Various other events have evolved as a direct result of the success of the Ryder Cup matches and are played along roughly similar lines. First came the contest between the club professionals of America and Great Britain and Ireland for the PGA Cup, often known as 'the Mini Ryder Cup'. Next came the Solheim Cup for the lady professionals of Europe and America. Not wanting to be left out, an international team, chosen from outside of Europe, was assembled to take on America in the Presidents Cup. Even this year, a new event was started in which a team representing Great Britain and Ireland take on a team from (Continental) Europe for the Seve Ballesteros Trophy.

It is a unique honour to represent your country on the world's golfing stage but also important to remember the sportsmanship and goodwill that such events were originally set up to promote. Samuel Ryder, with his strong Christian beliefs, was a shining example of these ideals and we can only rejoice in the legacy he has left behind.

Bernard Gallacher OBE
Wentworth
July 2000

Introduction

SAMUEL RYDER is world famous as the generous benefactor of golf's greatest team event – the Ryder Cup. He is also known as the successful businessman who launched his career as a seed merchant with his 'penny packets' of seeds. Until now, little else has been published of this remarkable man and yet Samuel Ryder was a good samaritan to the community and the greatest sponsor of British professional golf in the 1920s.

The author's special interest in Samuel Ryder started when he met Samuel's eldest daughter Marjorie twenty years ago while researching the history of his home golf club. He had heard that Samuel had regularly visited Came Down Golf Club in the years leading up to the founding of the Ryder Cup and wished to know more. By this time Marjorie Claisen was well into her eighties and living in Harpenden. She fondly recalled the family's visits to Dorset and went into her attic to produce an unframed picture of her father in mayoral robes. She then asked for it to be presented to Came Down Golf Club in memory of the family's happy association with the club. The club had the picture professionally cleaned and framed and it now hangs proudly in a prominent position in the club lounge.

Since then the author has met other members of the Ryder family and researched diligently in various books, newspapers, magazines and catalogues. His researches have unearthed a wealth of information, much of it previously unpublished, in order to present this first in-depth biography of Samuel Ryder. Many examples of Samuel's unique character are featured that highlight his generosity, compassion, determination, ingenuity and his keen sense of humour.

It is interesting to record that it was a breakdown in his health that led to Samuel Ryder being introduced to the game of golf. This proved to be a fortunate turn of events as Samuel went on to serve the game most generously from his base at Verulam Golf Club.

Various myths and suppositions have been put forward as to how the Ryder Cup event started. The author has carried out a thorough investigation of the facts as chronicled by authoritative newspapers and magazines of the 1920s. Accordingly the precise manner of the various events that led to Samuel Ryder presenting the Ryder Cup are thoroughly detailed. He rightly derived great pride in instituting this international sporting event. Little did he realize back in the 1920s what a huge commercial undertaking the event would become by the end of the twentieth century. As to what degree he would have approved is debatable but his principal desire remains that the highest standards of sportsmanship and fellowship endure between the two respective teams.

It is the author's wish that Samuel Ryder can now be accorded his true place in history. As a gentleman of the front rank, his contribution to society has been immense and the manner in which he always conducted himself is an example to everyone.

1

Early Years

SELDOM DO you discover someone who has gained respect from everyone in all the avenues of their life. However Samuel Ryder was one such man. No one had a cross word to say about him whether it was in connection with business, religion, sport or public life. Even his political opponents came to appreciate the honesty and fair play that Ryder stood for.

Rarely has anyone contributed so much to society in general. His generosity and ingenuity left gardens transformed, golf engraved with its greatest team event and St Albans refreshed with his years of noble public service.

Photographs of Samuel Ryder portray him as a Victorian gentleman of around six feet in height with a rather bushy moustache. He invariably wore a smart suit together with a tie or cravat as it suited him. A matching waistcoat containing a fob watch was an essential part of his outfit as were shiny black shoes. For outdoors a warm overcoat and a trademark homburg hat would complete the picture. Occasionally he would be seen smoking a pipe and sometimes he would have the family dog in tow. For watching a golf tournament he would have a shooting stick at the ready though later this was discarded for a more permanent walking stick.

His overall appearance make him out to be a somewhat grim-faced and serious individual. The perception was misleading as, in reality, he was generous, compassionate and full of humour.

The strong moral beliefs which sustained him throughout his life were gained by a strict Christian upbringing from the moment he was born. This took place on 24th March 1858 at Walton-le-Dale, a village just outside Preston in Lancashire.

At the time his father is recorded as being a gardener who also rejoiced in the name of Samuel. Work had taken him north with his dressmaker wife Elizabeth and two young daughters, Sarah and Ann. At Walton a third daughter Elizabeth arrived before Samuel Junior made his entrance into the world.

Samuel Ryder in characteristic pose

Samuel Senior was a descendant of a Shropshire family which contained some interesting ancestry. One great-great-uncle was intent on the good life come what may. He was said to have drank and gambled away the Ryder estates. As long as he could have his fill of port and underdone steaks, he was content. Things went downhill so much that his thoroughbred horses were led away to be sold in order to pay off his debts. He watched this activity quite unconcerned as he took up his accustomed position with his gouty foot resting on a stool.

A favourite family ancestor was one Lieutenant Ryder who was a Roundhead in Cromwell's army. He, too, by all accounts, fell foul of the high life and was summarily dismissed by Cromwell. Not to be deterred, he promptly galloped off and joined the army of King Charles. In the initial attack of the subsequent battle Lieutenant Ryder was the first officer to fall victim fighting for the King. Later family dissertations on the matter display the Ryder humour by saying how typical it was for a Ryder to be so absent-minded as to stick his head out!

The female side of the family also had its share of characters but one in particular stands out. A grandmother of Elizabeth's was a keen embroiderer who left behind her an attractive sampler displaying her name 'Susan Swallow'. More pertinently she ran a poultry farm with her husband and carried on the business despite his death. With the protective assistance of a gun with which she was adept, she would ward off unwanted intruders especially when they were in search of turkeys for Christmas. One night some of the village lads decided to set a surprise for her. On completion of one of her night patrols, she found a ghostly figure dressed in white, with a hollowed-out turnip and a candle for a head. Calm as could be, she walked towards the figure and blew out the candle which she put in her pocket. Then she coolly folded up the sheet and walked indoors. That incident well and truly established Susan's reputation. Apparently she was a Quakeress, so how gun-carrying squares up with that is a moot point!

The birth certificate of Samuel Ryder

Young Samuel was three years old when the family moved to Sale in Cheshire. Initially they moved into a house in Washway Road and Samuel Senior continued in the gardening business. Over the next few years the family was enlarged by the arrival of two girls, Jane and Mary, and two boys, James and John.

Sale is a suburb on the southern outskirts of Manchester which faced a tough existence at the time. The township was referred to as having a monotonously flat location and the most woefully dark place imaginable. Accordingly the local authorities were urged to rectify the scarcity of lamps as soon as possible. Roads were described as being ruinous and dangerous. They were forever being repaired, even the better roads surfaced with shale. Houses were modest and built to reflect the standing of the people who occupied them, ranging from first to fifth-class houses.

It was a time of industrial unrest and much desperate poverty prevailed. As a youngster Samuel used to go with his mother taking food to people, ill or out of work, who were really hungry. It was before the days of the welfare state and it had a profound effect on Samuel that was to stay with him forever. He determined there and then that if he was ever able to employ people they never should be penniless and hungry because they were ill.

3

Samuel Ryder Senior with his wife Elizabeth

During young Samuel's school days, the education picture nationally was undergoing important changes. In 1870 education was made compulsory and fees had to be paid. Parents who were too poor to pay had to apply to the Poor Law Guardians but by 1872 education had become free. The fundamental requisites were reading, writing and arithmetic. Candidates for schoolteachers had to understand the theory and practice of mensuration, have a good hand and read correctly.

Schools were divided mostly between those termed as being 'British' and those termed as being 'National'. A 'British' school was run under the auspices of the British and Foreign School Society with dissenting patronage and worked on the basis of non-denominational Bible teaching. By contrast, the 'National' schools were organised in line with Church of England practices under the name of the National Society for the Education of the Poor.

The Ryder children, brought up as Wesleyan Methodists, could have been sent to the Sale township school run as a 'British' school. However their parents decided otherwise and the children attended a local private school requiring the payment of school fees.

An even more important aspect of life was attendance at Sunday school. The Ryder children went to the Wesleyan Sunday school in School Road which had the added benefit of a lending library.

The adjoining Wesleyan chapel on the site of the present Boots Chemist enjoyed increasing attendances at this time. For many years Samuel Senior was one of the most gifted and talented preachers at the chapel and a regular Sunday school teacher in addition. Always he attended the weekly evening service and was on the Wesleyan Methodist Plan.

A caretaker for the chapel lived in the adjacent house. Apart from cleaning and maintenance, it was his responsibility to help keep order in the gallery on a Sunday. Collections were made quarterly and the funds

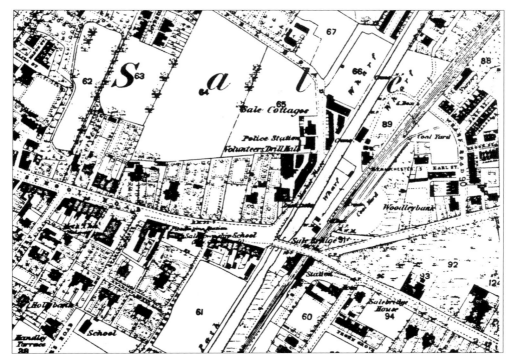

Map showing Sale in the 1870's

were used to finance extensions to the chapel and to improve the education in schools upholding the Wesleyan faith.

The chapel was well-known for its work with children's education. As a seventeen-year-old, young Samuel was impressed with this character-building process and was taken on as a junior Sunday school teacher in the fore-front of this activity. One important outcome was the Magic Lantern Group which comprised a club for young ladies and young gentlemen – effectively the forerunner of the modern youth club.

Another product of the chapel's endeavours was the Sale and District Musical Society. It was probably this organisation that helped to nurture young Samuel's love of music. His musical knowledge was further en-lightened by visits to Manchester's Free Trade Hall. As teenagers, Samuel and his brothers considered it a favourite pastime to save their pennies in order to hear Sir Charles Halle conducting orchestras and choirs.

Another entertainment which Samuel enjoyed was seeing plays per-formed in the local music hall. In particular he later fondly recollected seeing a short play called 'Editha's Burglar' with Albert Chevalier, the great Cockney actor and comedian, appearing as the burglar. Editha, a little girl, comes downstairs in her dressing-gown and begs the burglar not to take the

The streets around the Ryder family home in the late nineteenth century

candlesticks as they belonged to her mummy who had gone to heaven. The burglar replaces his loot and creeps away. The audience was greatly moved with not a dry eye in the house! What Samuel especially remembered was being amused that even the policeman on duty at the door was moved to tears.

From an early age Samuel was interested in sport. Rugby and cricket played important roles in his youth. He frequently played rugby and later boasted in jocular fashion of having been kicked in every part of his body. By comparison he regarded soccer as being very tame. However his greatest sporting passion as a youngster was with the game of cricket. In Sale that was especially appropriate as it is believed that the place name Sale is derived from the Anglo-Saxon word 'sealh' meaning the willow (from which cricket bats are made).

The family's move to Wharf Road in the 1860s brought Samuel to live just around the corner from the Sale Cricket and Quoits Club in Broad Road. He became fascinated with cricket and gradually gained the reputation of being a lob bowler of no mean distinction on the cricket fields of the north. For the best part of thirty years, he occasionally made use of the opportunity of seeing some of the best cricket at the nearby Old Trafford Ground, home to the Lancashire County Cricket Club.

At school Samuel proved a studious pupil with mathematics turning

Owen's College

out to be his favourite subject, for which he gained various distinctions. Examination success enabled him to enter Owens College, now more commonly known as part of Manchester University. There it was his aim to study for the teaching profession but he was later forced to abandon the idea. Intensive studies proved too much for a less than strong constitution. Poor health was to trouble him from time to time throughout his life.

Denied his intended career, Samuel joined a firm of Manchester shipping merchants where he spent several years gaining valuable experience. Suitably ingrained into the ways of business, he then joined his father's concern.

After acquiring a good deal of specialist knowledge, Samuel Senior had decided to set up a market garden business in 1865 and called it 'Ryder and Son'. He erected nurseries at the end of Wharf Road on a large plot of land behind the family home. The house was pulled down years ago and the nurseries have changed from those of horticultural use to those of children's use today.

Originally the business was quite a modest affair. The Ryders acted as nurserymen, seedsmen and florists chiefly for the benefit of Sale's influx of middle-class citizens. The location and timing of the business were important elements to the success of the venture. The premises were situated conveniently for a variety of transport systems. Within half a mile one could

The Ryder family pictured in Wharf Road in 1874 with sixteen-year-old Samuel seated in front

take advantage of the Bridgewater Canal, the new station at Sale Moor or main road links to Manchester. The immediate neighbours were a coal wharf, a warehouse and a timber yard making the area an important industrial site.

Samuel Senior was regarded as a gentleman of the front rank and a thoroughly practical man upon whose advice and opinion it was always wise to act. In his own particular sphere of horticulture he was recognised as the highest authority around. He was responsible for the design and layout of one of the most beautiful parks in Sale. His expertise was honoured with membership of the Royal Horticultural Society.

The construction of the railways created a demand for skills that made nearby Manchester the centre of the world's engineering industry. Coupled with the importance of the cotton industry, a wealthier influence comprising entrepreneurs and professional people moved into the area. Sale's population rapidly expanded. Urbanisation carried on apace and the price of land rose dramatically.

Into this tide of progress a mania grew up for gardening which ideally suited the Ryder business. A Sale magazine of 1868 aptly sets the scene:-

'The amount of gardening which may be observed in the course of an evening's walk is truly startling. For the first year of any individual's residence he is prepared to go to any

'Stowey' – the family house in Broad Road

length in the satisfaction of his new delight. He leaves his bed at unearthly hours in the morning. Then he boasts diligently and loudly all day in town on the subject. Wives and daughters, however, are equally enthusiastic. Watering the garden is their special forte. This operation they carry on at all costs, and in every description of weather.'

Samuel Senior was suitably impressed by his son's business acumen and quickly took him into the management side of the firm. With his ingenuity, Samuel Junior succeeded in building up a commercial undertaking of considerable importance with primulas being his special interest. Certainly business must have improved, for the family moved once more into a large detached house on the corner of Wharf Road and Broad Road. They named their new home 'Stowey' after Elizabeth Ryder's Somerset birthplace and, which, over 100 years later, still stands today as a private hotel.

Despite the family business being on an upward trend, Samuel Junior wanted to introduce fresh ideas to which his father declined to accede. Accordingly he left Sale and became associated with a big London retail house for which Samuel was asked to start a special branch of their business. Still not content, he then journeyed to Bolsover in Derbyshire where he acted as the manager for a large limited liability concern.

Whilst in Derbyshire he was frustrated to find that there were not the facilities for Nonconformists to which he had been accustomed. Not to be daunted, he continued to take a keen interest in religious matters by assisting the local Church of England vicar with his parish work.

Meanwhile his brothers and sisters were making their ways in the world. His brother James became a schoolmaster and the youngest brother John became apprenticed to a cabinet maker. No less than four of the sisters followed their mother into dressmaking. The exception was Marie, the youngest, who became a teacher at a high grade girls school run on a government basis.

Samuel's sister Jane married a doctor and, as can happen, became known as 'Jenny' for some strange reason. What many thought stranger still was that she became one of the early suffragettes. Jenny was furious that women had so little say in the upbringing of their children. For the father to have the legal right to make the important decisions and the mother's wishes to be ignored, Jenny considered absolutely wrong. Thus motivated, she decided to take up the cause.

Jenny took up a prominent position in the movement, even taking the chair at meetings addressed by Mrs. Emily Pankhurst, the leader of the suffragettes. Nevertheless she believed in peaceful methods and was not one of the more militant supporters that chained themselves to the railings. She may have been a determined person but she was basically a gentle lady. Although her husband agreed with her aims, the effect was that he lost a number of his patients. People said, 'Why, his wife is one of those terrible suffragettes!' However as he was such a popular doctor, patients managed to forgive him the fact that he had such a disconcerting wife and eventually decided to rejoin him.

Samuel was into his thirties before he married Helen Mary Barnard on 20th November 1890. Another committed Nonconformist, Helen was the second daughter of William Barnard, a tailor and draper working out of Market Place at Bishops Stortford in Hertfordshire. In time, Helen became known as 'Nellie' within the family.

The wedding took place at Blake Hall which was the residence of Mr. F. Spooner Woodward, brother-in-law to the bride. For the occasion, Helen wore a dress of cream serge, trimmed with beaver, with hat and feather to match, and carried a magnificent bouquet, the gift of a Mrs. Walkden. The service was later solemnised to choral accompaniment at the nearby Great Saling Church near Braintree in Essex. The officiating vicar was the Rev. T. Elrington and the number of wedding presents came to over fifty.

Helen was a gifted musician. She could play the organ, the piano and the violin in addition to being a soprano singer of some note. Her love of organ music was developed during her attendance at Bishops Stortford

Congregational Church where she helped a blind organist in the services. Whilst there she also went to the same Bible class as the vicar's son, a young Cecil Rhodes – later to become known for founding Rhodesia.

Religion and music were not the only factors that Samuel and Helen had in common. Helen was also known for her kindness, her generosity, her courage, her sense of humour and her love of people. However she was a more forthright person than her husband and her special concern was a complete abhorrence of humbugs and shams.

Just married, Samuel determined to do his utmost so that one day, when he could afford it, he would treat himself to three wishes. The first would be a diamond ring for Helen, the second would be a Bechstein piano for their drawing room and the third, a trip to the Holy Land. In due course, Samuel would live to see all three wishes fulfilled.

Within a few years the patter of tiny feet was heard. Two daughters added sparkle to their lives with the birth of Marjorie in 1893 and Kathleen in 1895.

Meanwhile, in the mind of Samuel, an important scheme was being developed. He had travelled widely by this time among both English and Continental establishments, taking careful note of the methods adopted as he went. Samuel also realised there were only two firms in the entire country that sold seeds through the post at that time. The important point was that these seeds were being sold for prices between 1/- and 10/- per packet making them affordable only to the owners of large properties or estates.

As a result of these considerations, he conceived the idea of starting the novel form of business which was to prove so great a success. He chose to have popular packets of the best seeds – penny packets – and to advertise in two newspapers. One key philosophy of this approach was to make gardening come within the scope of working class folk who would then take a keen interest in making their gardens a veritable splash of colour. The financial possibilities were not lost on Samuel.

His policy was dominated by a sincere desire to make it commercially viable for the man or woman with limited garden space not only to purchase everyday varieties of flowers and vegetables, but to gain the added pleasure of cultivating rarer strains, which previously had been confined to the wealthier growers.

The ambitious Samuel later explained his intentions. He said, 'I made up my mind that the principle I decided to adopt for this business was a great commercial principle. My friends and the trade did not agree with me, and urged me not to venture in it at all. But I was confident that I was right, and, in spite of all these discouragements, determined to realise my dream.'

The remaining question was precisely where to launch the business.

2

Samuel the Seedsman

TWO YEARS of scheming and planning ended with Samuel's carefully reasoned decision to establish his business at St Albans in Hertfordshire.

St Albans had been a small city with a grand past. Originally it was the site of Verulamium which was one of the most important Roman towns in Britain. The town's most famous inhabitant Alban became the country's first Christian martyr when he defied the Romans and ended up buried at the top of the hill above the River Ver. Ever since the place has been a shrine of pilgrimage. Another citizen of note was Lord Francis Bacon, the writer and philosopher. For years St Albans was one of the most important staging posts on the main road from London to the north and, although this element has been lost, the important local market still prospers to this day.

When Samuel arrived, industry in St Albans was mainly traditional and agriculture-based. Straw hat making was booming and boaters were a fashionable speciality. Similarly the associated manufacture of straw trimmings and straw plaiting provided employment for many people. Additionally there was a silk mill, two breweries, maltings, two boot factories, a brush factory and a clothing factory. For better or, for some, worse was the fact that as many as ninety public houses provided temptation and so kept the local magistrates' bench busy with charges of drunkenness.

Samuel's resolve to set up in Hertfordshire coincided with his father's withdrawal from the world of horticulture. Samuel Senior sold his Cheshire premises for a retirement which lasted for some nine years until his death at the age of eighty.

An important reason for Samuel's choice of location took in the fact that St Albans had a very small population and therefore probably apportioned low rents and low rates. However his principal concern was that his business would be predominantly a postal business. That being so, he realized that the city's three railway stations would ensure speedy postal delivery to all parts of the country. In Samuel's own words, 'I began in St Albans because, from my point of view, it is the centre of the Kingdom. As mine is a postal business, that is very important.'

Once resident in St Albans, Samuel's next move was to consult town directories in the local library. In this way he was able to deduce the poorer areas of towns and duly noted down appropriate names and addresses. In tandem with this, he compiled an attractive seed catalogue in the knowledge that he could buy his supplies wholesale. Despite having no sons himself, he called the business 'Ryder and Son' as a tribute to his father. He used the slogan that became his byword in horticulture, 'All seeds in penny packets from orchids to mustard and cress'.

With his wife's help, they got busy addressing the labels on the wrappings for 250 catalogues. Then they proceeded to carry the completed catalogues in a large laundry basket to the main post office a mile distant. Several such trips were necessary to complete the task. Each catalogue was posted for the equivalent of a half penny for they could all be sent off as a batch of circulars which kept the price down.

This activity took place on a Friday with the intention that the working man would receive the catalogue in Saturday morning's post. Being most people's half day at the time, Samuel's aspiration was that respondents would fill out the order form and attach the necessary number of stamps to complete the order. The orders would be sent off over the weekend so that Samuel would get them on the following Monday.

According to his eldest daughter Marjorie, Friday's operations left Samuel with just 2/6d in the whole world which he put into the collection plate at Sunday morning service. It is hard to believe that a family man would give away his last penny in this way but the story does indicate Samuel's great confidence in the eventual success of his enterprise.

His trust was vindicated on the Monday morning. Orders, accompanied by unused stamps, started to filter in enabling Samuel to buy the necessary seeds and printed packets. During the week he and his wife would sort the seeds into penny packets within the confines of a small shed. Then, with a speed of delivery for which they would become famous, they posted it off so that the customer would receive it in time for planting on his next day off.

The business had a humble start. Samuel acquired his first business premises in an upstairs room over a hatter's shop in the High Street. Realizing the kind of business he envisaged was entirely new, he began in a limited way with just himself and a boy. Before very long, Samuel had recruited another person and together they strived, for all their worth, to get the business firmly established.

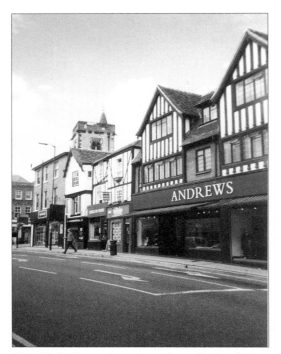

The High Street location where Ryder & Son started out

It was hard work but it was harder still during the second season when it had been demonstrated to a critical public that Ryders' 'Penny Packets' Seeds produced results at least as satisfactory as the ordinary high-priced packets available at the time. The public soon realized the value of the Ryder service and came to support the venture so whole-heartedly that, in time, success was assured.

Advertising played a key part in the growth of the business. Samuel later acknowledged that, without the various and consistent advertising campaigns undertaken by Ryders', the subsequent results would not have been possible.

By the time Ryders' was launched, St Albans already had in its midst high-class nurseries off Camp Road called St Albans Orchid Nurseries run by Messrs. Sanders. However it could not be considered a rival as Samuel explained, 'Messrs. Sanders appeals to what we may call the aristocrats of gardening, whereas my business is a business that appeals to the million, for whereas Messrs. Sanders will sell an orchid for 100 guineas and more, I sell my penny packets of mignonette.'

By 1897 larger premises were required and so the business moved to a site set between 11 and 13 Lower Dagnall Street. Samuel hired from one Joshua Pearce a disused chapel known as the Old Presbyterian Meeting House which dated back to 1697. For the expanding business, Samuel converted it for use as a seed warehouse complete with a loft for storage purposes.

For its previous use the congregation would have gathered in a rather dark interior. However there was a window high up in one of the walls where, at midday in fine weather, the sun would throw a bright beam which lighted up the whole place.

Samuel, with his Christian awareness, was convinced that the building was the inspiration for a well-known hymn. In the eighteenth century the

AN OLD MEETING HOUSE.

The Old Presbyterian Meeting House

young and often depressed poet William Cowper would regularly attend the chapel in the company of his psychiatrist Dr. Cotton. After one such visit Cowper wrote the following hymn,

> 'Sometimes a light surprises
> The Christian while he sings
> It is the Lord who rises
> With healing in his wing.
>
> When comforts are declining
> He grants the soul again
> A season of clear shining
> To cheer it, after rain.'

Like the founders of other successful businesses, success did not happen overnight. Samuel explained, 'In the early part of the business we met with very serious difficulties. Sometimes I thought we should never be able to do it. The extra labour beyond what is usual in the seed trade being so enormous in regard to the putting up of the seeds into packets.'

For five years Ryders' prospered at the Old Presbyterian Meeting House. Gradually more orders filtered in and necessitated the recruitment of addi-

The old Wesleyan chapel with the schoolroom to the left of the picture

tional staff to cope with the increased workload. Then in 1902 Samuel gave the premises back to Joshua Pearce and transferred the business to a still larger building just 100 yards up the road. This time he took over the old Wesleyan Sunday school building in Upper Dagnall Street.

The move was short-lived as Samuel realized that he required still bigger business premises. He went to St Albans' brightest young architect Percival Blow and asked him to find a site on which he could erect a warehouse to cope with his expanding business. Blow duly found a large site close to the city centre and made arrangements for the sale but without Samuel knowing about it for some while because he was suffering so terribly from whooping cough.

Accordingly, in the summer of 1903, Samuel acquired a residence at 27 Holywell Hill which was situated next door to the seventeenth century White Hart Inn made famous by Charles Dickens in 'The Pickwick Papers'. The grounds extended to nearly 50,000 square feet in which Samuel erected a sizeable building to the rear of the premises. The building constituted the largest warehouse in the city and was suitably equipped.

The experience of extreme poverty as a young man growing up in the Manchester area still preyed on his mind with the result that he became a real friend to his employees. He proved to be a pioneer in the welfare of staff and years ahead in ensuring employment conditions that later proved mandatory. Accordingly he exercised the greatest care in health and hygiene so that the people employed there were able to carry out their duties in the most pleasant of working environments. He even paid their wages when they had cause to be off sick. Fellow citizens were dismissive saying, 'Poor old Ryder, he'll soon discover that you can't trust people like that!' Nevertheless Samuel was never let down and evoked a special loyalty and respect that was mutual.

The business was a very popular one with the young women of St Albans who made up almost the entire work force. It is evident that Samuel was always appreciative of their assistance and once remarked,

C.G. Davis – General Manager of Ryder & Son

'I always say that my business has been made by the St Albans girls and I always say that the St Albans girls are gifted in their fingers.' Accordingly it is no surprise to hear that Samuel had no difficulty whatever in taking on the necessary staff. Indeed he asserted that he was able to get twenty applicants for each position available.

The country as a whole suffered a general depression in trade in 1904. However local commerce in St Albans was said to be in a flourishing state. Certainly Ryders' seemed to be bucking the national trend. By 1906 the firm's operation consisted of 5,000 varieties of seeds which were sent to every corner of the world. Some idea of the importance of the business can be deduced from the fact that in the season more than 2,000 orders were despatched on a daily basis.

The permanent staff then numbered between eighty to ninety, all of whom, except two, were girls who worked under the direction of the new manager. The manager in question was Charles George Davis. As the husband of Samuel's sister Marie, C. G. Davis had gained the respect of Samuel as both experienced businessman and gentleman. His presence not only would be a reassuring influence as the business continued to grow but would also enable Samuel to travel more in order to provide extra varieties for the firm's customers.

RYDERS' SEEDS

In Penny Packets are of the best quality. No matter what price you pay you cannot get better, and for a small sum you can have a splendid selection which will make your garden beautiful. Write to-day for a Catalogue, which will be sent **free**, with beautiful Coloured Plate, by return of post.

RYDER and SON,

Seed Specialists,

ST. ALBANS.

BEWARE of IMITATORS.

A 1909 advertisement for Ryder & Son

Business life did not always run smoothly. The firm's unique system of supplying seeds of the very finest flowers and vegetables in penny packets was the envy of others. A host of imitators unscrupulously attempted to reap a harvest from the public on the strength of the reputation that Ryders' had established for its seeds. Most of the claims to consideration put forward by these mushrooming concerns were so obviously untrue as to defeat their own object. Not only were their own catalogues closely imitated in colour, compilation and general appearance, but whole blocks of the text were maliciously taken from Ryders' catalogues. Daily, during the season, evidence was received from customers of these disreputable tactics. Samuel regarded these parasitic methods with complete calm for they could be construed as a compliment. His biggest concern was that the seeds distributed by these dubious operators were of such inferior quality that people would be prejudiced from buying 'penny packets' at all.

One such copycat company ended up in court. Samuel decided enough was enough and took an outfit calling itself the 'St Albans X L All Seed Company, Limited' to the Chancery Division of the High Court. This bogus concern with seven signatories registered themselves as a company with a nominal capital of £2,000. Although they had small premises in Leytonstone, their letterhead used the words 'The St Albans X L All Seed

Company, Ltd., seed merchants and growers, St Albans, England' and, furthermore, they copied paragraphs from the Ryders' catalogue word for word. They had the impudence to state on the very first page of their catalogue:- 'This company has been formed for the purpose of consolidating and extending the already large business in what is known as the 'Penny Packet Seed' trade, by direct supply.' Not surprisingly Mr. Justice Warrington found in favour of Ryders' and conferred a restraint of trade order on the offending company.

In 1910 Samuel added a new wing to the gigantic warehouse. However, only a year later, the continued expansion of the business rendered it imperative that additional premises be provided. Since he had acquired the plot off Holywell Hill, Samuel had used the inherited Edwardian offices fronting the main road as a part of his offices. After a few years of use, he considered them to be both inconvenient and insanitary. Accordingly Samuel decided to replace them with a new suite of offices more in keeping with the importance of the business and which was intended, at the same time, to constitute an ornament among the business premises of the city.

However he faced strong opposition from local antiquarians. The building in question had an interesting history. Prior to the building as Edwardian offices, it was a house known as the Priory and, before that, was originally the medieval Bull Inn. At one time this was considered to be one of the most famous coaching houses in England and it is on record that Queen Elizabeth I was once entertained there. The building was full of objects of antiquarian interest. In the foundations of the walls, there were built-in bottles of wine. Another unusual feature was that many of the timbers used in its construction had the appearance of having been old ship's timbers.

In reply to the criticism over preservation, Samuel commented, 'We have hesitated to destroy this old place but the time had arrived when our organisation must be improved and facilities must be provided for executing our business more rapidly. You will be able to form some conception of the growth of our business when I tell you that this year our turnover has increased 25% as compared with last year. I have as great a veneration for ancient buildings as anyone, but there is the commercial side of the city's welfare to be studied; and I look at it this way: Here is new business bringing thousands of pounds into the city every year, employing a great many young people, and giving work out in the city as well – to the printers and others – and surely that should be considered.'

Plans were therefore prepared, on Samuel Ryder's instructions, by St Albans' most respected architect Percival Blow. One of the lowest tenders for the building contract came from Messrs. C. Miskin and Son who were engaged to demolish the old house and erect the new offices for a sum described as being approximately £6,000.

At this time each development of a major building was celebrated with a grand ceremony for laying the foundation stone. Ryders' new building was no exception. Most of the staff, several members of the Ryder family and those associated with the project assembled on 21st July 1911 to witness the event.

Matters started with the careful positioning of a time capsule. Samuel considered that the new building would be built so substantially that it would last hundreds of years but whenever it was pulled down future generations should learn of the great business that had been carried on at that location. Into the cavity between the stones, he placed a sealed bottle containing on parchment a short history of the business, the latest Ryders' catalogue, a few packets of their seeds and some current coins of the realm. To complete the operation, two local newspapers were placed separately in the cavity.

Having placed the bottle and the newspapers in the cavity, Samuel covered them with a metal plate, upon which was engraved, 'This stone was laid on 21st July, 1911, by Mrs. Ryder, wife of Samuel Ryder, Esq., JP (proprietor). Percival C. Blow, ARIBA.'

The architect then handed to Helen Ryder a handsome silver trowel with ivory handle, with the inscription, 'Presented by Percival C. Blow, ARIBA, to Mrs. Samuel Ryder, on the occasion of the stone-laying of the offices, Holywell-Hill, St Albans, July 21st., 1911.' With this elegant tool, Mrs. Ryder spread the mortar upon one of the large Aberdeen granite blocks in true business-like fashion, and the next block was lowered into position. She tapped the stone at its four corners with a mallet, and having tested it with the spirit level, said, 'I declare this stone well and truly laid.' As a memento of the occasion, Samuel gave Helen a brooch with a facsimile of the trowel in gold with a pearl handle.

The ceremony ended with prayers from the Reverend F. H. Wheeler after which the assembled company adjourned for lunch to the Town Hall. Mr. T. Slater provided the catering there where a series of appropriate toasts was proposed.

Samuel, in a long speech, expressed satisfaction and pride that his enterprise gave delight to so many and so cheaply. He felt that he and those associated with him were not engaged merely in business but in something far greater. Strange as it may appear, although he liked to make money and liked the firm to progress, the greatest thing before his mind was the fact that he was doing something to cultivate the best tastes of men and women.

He had to congratulate himself and those around him upon having to do with a great commercial undertaking.

He considered that they might not make the amount of money out of it that some businesses make, but he very much questioned whether there was an operation in the wide world that touched so many parts of the world. He often received news of his business activities from distant lands. He had a lady at his house one day and she said she had been to Jerusalem, where she saw a most beautiful garden and the seeds came from his firm. If Sir Ernest Shackleton or someone ever discovered the South Pole, he was quite confident someone would come and say to him, 'Do you know, Mr. Ryder, when we were at the South Pole we found that the people there knew all about you, and winding round the South Pole was a beautiful garland of flowers raised from your seeds?' That was one way of saying how the business reached nearly every region of the world.

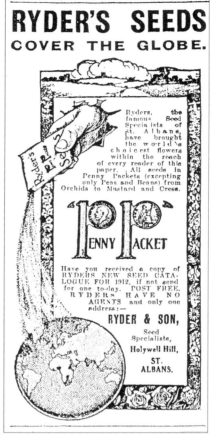

A 1912 advertisement for Ryder & Son

Showing obvious sympathy with the suffragette movement, Samuel confessed that if he were offered a staff of men as compared with a staff of women, he would prefer the staff of women. He continued to praise all his staff. In his brother-in-law (C. G. Davis) he had a manager who, he was sure, was esteemed and admired by every one of their employees. Samuel Lucas, the head of the seed department, came to him as a bright, intelligent boy and said he had become a man who had acquired an unrivalled specialist knowledge of gardening. He described Samuel Buttenshaw as one of the best accountants in the land whose knowledge of book-keeping and love of figures were phenomenal.

In the course of demolishing the old building it was discovered that it was in a more decayed state than was realized. In its place a magnificent suite of new offices was erected in keeping with the commercial architecture of the city. A fine treatment of the Georgian style was adopted and executed in red brick with Bath stone dressings. The date of construction was identified by the year '1911' set over the main entrance. The facade was embellished with two carved stone bas-reliefs. One depicted men ploughing and sowing and the other showed women harvesting. The main approach was through a massive central stone doorway with a semi-circular arch supported on pillars. This opened into a lobby which, in turn, led into a sumptuous mahogany and oak furnished entrance hall with parquet floor and dome. Leading out of this hall on the same level were found the important postal department, the general manager's office, the sales office and the typing pool.

A grand mahogany staircase led to Samuel's private office which combined the accommodation of a library and a study. The main feature of the room was a grand fireplace with the initials 'SR' carved into the mahogany Edwardian surround, decorated with elaborate harvest imagery. To complete matters, Samuel hung a splendid oil painting entitled 'Undaunted' on the wall of his office. It showed an old gardener tending his plants in his greenhouse with broken glass and derelict buildings in the background.

Staff were provided with cloakrooms, lavatories and bicycle sheds in the basement. Another part of the scheme saw the warehouse extended so as to communicate directly with the new offices. The premises were fully illuminated by electric light and heated by radiators.

Alongside the building an elaborate cast iron gateway was erected proudly displaying 'Ryder & Son' within its design. Through this gateway all deliveries and supplies were then transported. Samuel also bought the two properties between the gateway and Albert Street with the view to future expansion of the business.

The opening ceremony for the completed development took place on Monday 18th December 1911. This time there was little in the way of formalities. Samuel's youngest daughter Joan, aged just seven, was given the honour of starting the proceedings. Punctually at ten o'clock in the morning, she arrived in her father's Rolls Royce with some friends and pushed open the massive front doors. Then she walked through into the sales office and made a purchase of seeds for her own garden with a sixpence. The chief cashier presented her, as the first customer to visit the new offices, with a written receipt for this amount enclosed in a handsome morocco case. He, in turn, kept the sixpence in order to have it framed for posterity. The presentation of a bouquet followed before the party was taken on a guided tour of the buildings. Having spent a very pleasant hour going round the premises, they left after expressing their satisfaction with the arrangements and wishing the firm all prosperity.

Regrettably, within days of completion, the new offices suffered damage

Samuel Ryder with the builders' foreman during the building of his Holywell Hill offices

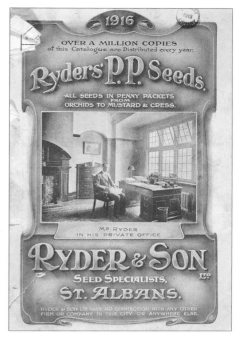

The back cover of Ryders' catalogue for 1916 showing Samuel Ryder in his private office (Royal Horticultural Society, Lindley Library)

Line drawing of the Ryder & Son premises on Holywell Hill

The staff at Ryders' busy at work (Reproduced by kind permission of Carrington and Richardson, Copyright reserved)

at the hands of unruly youngsters. They not only broke some of the tinted glass windows in the front but also filled up the letter-box with gravel and stones.

Shortly after local historian Gilbert Oakley in a lecture to the St Albans Debating Society expressed confidence in how the city was developing and asked for a more positive outlook from the city's citizens. With possibly one eye on Ryder and Son, he advised them in verse:-

> 'Speak with the voice of conviction,
> We'll reap just what we sow,
> Spread the praise of St Albans,
> And watch St Albans grow.'

Ryders' experienced extraordinary difficulties during the years of the First World War. They had to cope with the scarcity of seeds, the difficulty of transport and the shortage of labour. Accordingly it was inevitable that prices increased. Nevertheless the amount of business practically doubled during the war. Concerned at his limited supply, Samuel spent a good deal of time abroad discovering new and productive sources so that he could provide plenty of varieties of first-class, high quality seeds for his customers. His best results were obtained during visits to British Columbia and California.

The war meant food shortages and a famine in potatoes resulted. The potatoes that were available were prone to serious disease putting a premium on them. After the war Ryders' took this problem into consideration and conducted experiments with 2,500 seedlings laid out in two-and-a-half acres of land next to Samuel's home at Marlborough House. Their research resulted in the development of hybridized potato seeds free of disease. This was widely acclaimed not only as a horticultural success but as a great benefit to the nation at large. Ryders' encouraged this progress with a successful hybrid potato show of their own complete with cash prizes.

By 1920 Ryders' were distributing over a million copies of their catalogue all over the world. Frequently it was the case that over 10,000 orders were processed and despatched between 8 a.m. and 8 p.m. in the course of an ordinary day's business requiring about 100 mail sacks of small packets. It was therefore no surprise that in the same year the firm became a limited company. Its shares were held almost entirely by the directors, the employees and the customers.

Alongside Samuel as directors of the new limited company were Charles G. Davis, Thomas Seaton and Edward Conway. Samuel Buttenshaw retired in December 1920 from his position as company secretary to be replaced by John Taylor Wincap. Amongst the female staff, Miss Nevell became Samuel's personal private secretary and another employee, with nursing experience, was able to render first aid whenever required. Additionally long-serving Mrs. Elizabeth Stratton was the reliable charlady.

The demand for Ryders' seeds increased to such an extent that it necessitated the acquisition of further storage space. Most of this was found 100 yards up the road in premises next to 3 Holywell Hill. The building was approached through a wide tunnel-like entrance originally designed to take a horse and coach into an inn yard. The stables, tack rooms and hay lofts were ideal for conversion to use as stores.

Amongst the world of horticulture it was recognised that Messrs. Ryder and Son had become a very highly organised business representing value and promptness. Only the best quality seeds would do effecting the slogan 'Nothing is too good for Ryders'. It was the firm's proud boast that it sent 'Seeds by Return' so a twenty-four hour turnaround became the norm.

Each order was treated with the most scrupulous care and attention. The envelope was opened and the order scrutinized by a highly-trained official. Passing along, it was again checked and diverted to its proper place in the despatching department. Here the items were collected together by a

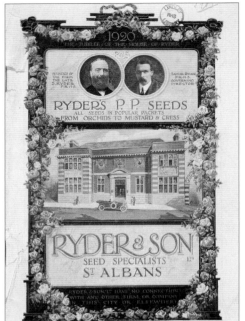

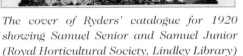

The cover of Ryders' catalogue for 1920 showing Samuel Senior and Samuel Junior (Royal Horticultural Society, Lindley Library)

A colourful advertisement for Ryders' Seeds (Reproduced by kind permission of St. Albans Museums, copyright reserved)

trained staff, who did nothing else but this kind of work. The order was passed along and again checked, and finally reached a despatcher, who ticked the order, wrote the label and passed the whole forward to a packer, who made ready for post, rail or steamer as necessary.

There was a unique feature about the order department. It operated a quadrupling of the despatching system, so that four distinct groups of orders by four separate staffs were executed at the same time.

Ryders' 'Post Office' was another department, through which thousands of packages travelled rapidly, the GPO vans calling four times daily. Once Samuel did not avail himself of the GPO. Samuel objected to the high postal rates prevalent in 1922 and made a remarkable protest. By his shrewdness, he discovered that he could post his catalogue lists in Leipzig, Germany for one quarter of the cost in Great Britain. It being legally necessary for the matter to be printed in the country where posted, it was set in type in England and 'impressed' abroad. The issue got to the ears of an MP who subsequently raised the matter in the House of Commons.

Nearly 300 staff were on the payroll at this time with 200 engaged in the packing department. Thanks to Samuel's instructions, the nearly all female staff had a break of thirty minutes every morning for community singing, supported by an organ. That was one of the sympathetic sides of Samuel's character.

Samuel realised by now that there were demands on the business if he was to remain fully competitive in the horticultural world. Accordingly he decided not to rely solely on seeds any more and started to diversify. He introduced floral perfumes and changed his catalogues to include bulbs as well as seeds.

Some of the front covers for his catalogues were truly works of art. He became aware of an artist by the name of Miss Winifred Walker. He noticed a painting of 'Wallflowers' that she exhibited at the Royal Academy of Art in 1925 and decided

Examples of the Ryder catalogues adorned by Winifred Walker paintings

to buy it. He then arranged for it to adorn one of his catalogues. This had such a good response that he arranged for more of her floral pictures to front his catalogues in succeeding years. Accordingly 'Everybody's Flowers', 'Anemones', 'A Bouquet from an Old-World Garden' and 'Pewter Pot' followed in turn. He encouraged orders by sending copies of the paintings free with orders over £1 in value.

A particular speciality of Ryders' was sweet peas. They became famous for their many varieties and Samuel decided to name some of them after friends and relatives. His wife and three daughters were amongst those so honoured along with the famous golf professional Abe Mitchell and Mrs. Mitchell. Samuel even used his own name but this time it was for a dainty variety of free-flowering primula called 'Novelty Primula Stellata Samuel Ryder'.

Ryders' naturally developed links with organisations in the horticultural world. It was no surprise that allotment associations enjoyed a close affiliation but it was the various horticultural societies that provided mutual respect and gain for that matter. Samuel himself was president of the local St Albans Horticultural Society for a term presenting a large challenge cup for the best group of plants.

SWEET PEAS.

NEW SWEET PEA
JOAN RYDER
Catalogue No. 5346.

The finest White

Sweet Pea of the year. Joan Ryder has appeared in all the leading exhibits at the principal shows throughout the country and has received many awards. Per packet, 6d. and 1/-

NEW SWEET PEA
MARJORIE RYDER
Catalogue No. 5348.

The finest Crimson.

Described by one of the leading Sweet Pea Specialists as the " only " Crimson Sweet Pea—a fine companion to No. 5346. Per packet, 6d. and 1/-

NEW SWEET PEA
NELLIE RYDER
Catalogue No. 5347.
The finest Cerise.

The colour can only be described as rich cherry cerise quite distinct. Flowers large, wonderfully waved standard, and delightfully fringed wings, a grand exhibition and garden variety. Per packet, 6d. and 1/-

NEW SWEET PEA
KITTY RYDER
Catalogue No. 5349.
The finest Rose Pink.

This variety is salmon in the bud, developing later into a rich rosy cream pink ; flowers remarkably large, well waved and frequently double. Glorious for exhibition or garden, and especially beautiful when cut. Per packet, 6d. & 1/-

Varieties of sweet peas named after members of the Ryder family

Indeed Samuel led the way in staging exhibitions and shows. At his Holywell Hill premises he put on various vegetable shows and flower shows. For a while Ryders' gained many big prizes at approved horticultural shows. In 1923 Samuel changed tack. He opted out of entering competitions and put up various prizes himself at these shows to those of the winning exhibitors who had used Ryders' seeds. Initially these prizes were in the form of cash but later included a Ryder silver challenge cup for the year's best exhibitor and Ryder gilt medals. Additionally he put up cash prizes for quality photographs of horticultural subjects.

As the business continued to grow, Samuel decided to erect an exhibition hall on the vacant plot that he had bought years before between the firm's driveway and Albert Street. With this venture, Samuel's aim was to have a perpetual showpiece throughout the season to display examples of Ryders' specialities in flowers and vegetables for the garden.

Once again Samuel called in Percival Blow as his architect and Messrs. C. Miskin and Sons as the builders. They erected a glazed exhibition hall that was described by one observer as a 'Crystal Palace' in miniature. The hall was constructed of reinforced brick and concrete, treated internally and externally with a special cream cement. It was around fifty-five feet square with substantial supporting pillars. The floor was made up of specially made tiles of the same tint as the walls and the contrast produced

The newly-opened Ryders' Exhibition Hall

The interior of the Ryders' Exhibition Hall

Samuel Ryder inside the exhibition hall

by the ornamental window frames broke up the severe lines of the structure. Careful consideration was given to heating and ventilation so that plants and flowers should remain fresh for as long as possible. Within the exhibition hall, 3,000 feet of floor space were arranged tastefully with a magnificent display of flowers taken from Ryders' seeds. A sundial, a fountain and attractive garden furniture completed the display.

The opportunity was taken at the same time to set up a germinating room in an adjoining building. This would enable seeds to be tested under the most ideal conditions.

The new establishment was opened formally on 6th May 1931 before a gathering made up of notable figures of the horticultural world and the press. At the lunch which followed, Samuel's foresight was praised to such effect that he would make an ideal member of the Publicity Committee of the Royal Horticultural Society.

By this time Charles Davis had retired to Sussex and Edward Conway had also left the board of directors. A great friend of Samuel's then proceeded to take his place as a director. Stanley Robinson had been acting as the firm's solicitor for some time and had travelled with Samuel on trips abroad. Robinson was also a prominent citizen being secretary of the local chamber of commerce for many years and a local councillor for a while. Although

Ryders' trial grounds at Roe Hyde

their political allegiances were distinctly at variance, they appreciated each other's fair play and got on well together. By 1933 Thomas Seaton had also left the board and Samuel appointed Martin Jenkins to replace him. Samuel was seventy-five years old by now so, maybe with the future in mind, he also appointed his youngest daughter Joan to be a director.

Diversification of the business carried on apace. The varieties of flowers and vegetables on offer continued to increase but shrubs, fruit trees, manure, fertilizers, slug killers, worm eradicators, lawn invigorators and grass seed were among those items added. Samuel was determined to provide more and more for the gardener such as aids like sprayers, cold frames, cloches, training nets for peas and beans and even a gardener's diary.

Further progress for the firm came with the acquisition in 1934 of an extensive plot of land at Roe Hyde situated between the North Orbital Road and the Barnet By-Pass. The site was adapted for use as trial grounds in order to grow flowers and vegetables for seed and nursery stock for sale. A grand driveway was constructed along with suitable greenhouses, warehouses and sheds. Vans were purchased and additional staff taken on to operate this new branch of the business. Sadly Samuel was to witness only one year of this new development.

3

Religious Foundation

AMUEL'S PRIMARY interest and foundation in life was his Christian com
mitment. His eldest daughter Marjorie once remarked that without
ever preaching to his daughters, Samuel set them an example of
Christian living which one only comes across once or twice in a lifetime.

When Samuel was in business in Dagnall Street, he only had to go just
round the corner to attend the Independent Chapel in Spicer Street. This
chapel had been the focal point for Congregationalists in the city since
1812. On arrival in St Albans, the family quickly decided that it suited their
strong Nonconformist beliefs and regularly attended services there. Samuel
became a most influential member of this chapel and was made one of the
team of ten deacons within a short time.

As Nonconformists they were considered Dissenters and, to some in a
cathedral city, that was the equivalent of second-class citizens. The Spicer
Street chapel was a typical example of the chapels that had been planted
throughout the country in modest, humble places away from the main
thoroughfares. The lords of the manor would not accede to their erection
in the High Streets of the towns but by their very numbers and patronage
they were a power in the land.

Sermons, often of an hour or so in duration, took a very important part
in their Sunday morning services. The discourses were given by devoted and
inspiring preachers who could draw and hold crowds which listened with
respect and endurance. The enthralled congregation came to appreciate
their inheritance and thereby enjoy the religious freedom which was the
great benefit. It was an age when the morning sermon was the chief topic
of conversation at Sunday dinner-time. If one had not listened properly one
cut a poor figure in the discussion.

In reality there was a hard line drawn between Church and Chapel
causing great competition between the denominations. Church of England
people dealt with Church of England tradesmen and Nonconformist people

dealt with Nonconformist trades-men. This rivalry even showed up in the habits of the shopping frater-nity. For example it was a definite practice in the Ryder family to buy groceries from Mr. Greenfield, a member of the Baptist Tabernacle. They wouldn't dream of getting drapery from Mr. Green, a church warden at the Abbey, when Mr. Watson, a fellow Congregationalist, had his little shop in Holywell Hill.

The religious education of children was a contentious issue at the turn of the century and accen-tuated the differences between the main strands of Christian beliefs. Sympathetic to the passive resist-ance movement, Samuel was responsible for organising several meetings aimed at opposing the education acts to be put before

Spicer Street Independent Chapel

Parliament. In this matter he persuaded prominent speakers like Dr. John Clifford and the Rev. Charles Sylvester Horne to address meetings in St Albans.

Samuel held strong views regarding the religious education of children and was especially critical of the churches' lack of guidance for children. He continually argued that they neither spent enough nor did enough for the children in this regard. This topic became his 'annual grumble' which he repeated at every anniversary gathering. Samuel played his part with his enthusiastic support of the work done by Sunday school education. Very soon he was made the assistant superintendent at the Spicer Street chapel and, in due course, superintendent. In 1901 he was responsible for supervising eighteen teachers and 310 scholars.

The Ryder family started attending the Spicer Street chapel at almost the same time as the Rev. William Carson arrived straight from Hackney College to start his pastorate. This former draper from Ballymena may have been young and inexperienced but was noted for his kind nature and strong Christian character. The Irishman had already impressed many with his preachings as a pulpit supply stand-in on several occasions and so was invited to become the minister. He quickly struck up a strong friendship with Samuel Ryder, which worked out to their mutual benefit.

Rev. Carson took a keen interest in political matters and was not afraid to speak his mind should he consider it appropriate. Not surprisingly he followed the Irish situation but, controversially, took a conciliatory stance on the Boer War issue. This attitude did not go down too well with some citizens who accused him of being 'pro-Boer'. Although of strong moral beliefs himself, it was Samuel Ryder's sensible advice that kept Rev. Carson's sermons from becoming too political in content.

It was a time when the principles of Nonconformity were undergoing a great upsurge. Improved literacy and a greater awareness of political matters were contributory factors in filling the churches with ever-increasing numbers. There was a growing need for bigger churches to cope with these numbers.

In addition the rapidly expanding population of the Victorian era made constant demands on small and old-fashioned churches such as the chapel in Spicer Street. The migration of Londoners to St Albans gradually swelled the population of the city and a fair proportion of the new arrivals associated themselves with the Spicer Street chapel. Thus every year, and almost every month, the need for larger and more convenient headquarters became apparent.

The accommodation available at Spicer Street had become inadequate and it was no surprise that the Congregationalists should wish to obtain a new building for their work. Clearly the time had arrived when a church worthy of the denomination should be erected. This course of action was not unexpected as the Rev. Carson only accepted the pastorate after obtaining an undertaking from the members that they would seriously approach the question of building a new church.

A committee was set up in 1898 with the purpose of finding a suitable site. Rev. Carson took on the onerous task of summoning up sufficient interest in the project to make it a reality. In general the deacons were uncertain as to the best course of action but that was when Samuel Ryder stepped in. As a respected employer in the city, Ryder was an important figure who threw all his energies and influence into the cause. He had no doubt that they must press for a suitable site and go ahead with building as soon as possible.

Initially they planned to build on a vacant plot in Marlborough Road. However, they were too late for the Methodists had beaten them to it with an offer enabling them to erect their own new church.

Victoria Street in the 1900's showing Trinity Church to the right of the picture

Not to be daunted, Rev. Carson continued the search and an alternative site was found at the corner of Victoria Street and Beaconsfield Road. This site turned out to be ideal as the city was growing eastwards towards the Midland Railway station at the far end of Victoria Street. Shops were opening up nearby and it was inevitable that travellers emerging from the station would see the new church immediately opposite. Ultimately, as the result of prolonged and serious discussion, the scheme was finalized at a special church meeting in 1899 when the decision was made to purchase the site for £1,700.

Matters were not straightforward however and progress towards completion of the project was seriously delayed. Samuel Ryder was certainly the driving force that helped to keep the plans on track. In particular, his resolute attitude ensured that subscriptions continued to filter in as a further £9,000 was considered necessary to finance the building work. Samuel led the enthusiastic and generous response by example with two separate donations of £100.

The architects Messrs. Smee, Mence and Houchin drew up the plans and a tender for the building work was accepted from the well-known local firm of Messrs. C. Miskin and Sons. The builders eventually moved on to the site in May 1902 and a grand stone-laying ceremony took place during the

Trinity Congregational Church

following July in the company of members of the city council. The development was finally completed in September of 1903.

The new edifice was named the Trinity Congregational Church and was the scene for a joyful opening ceremony on 8th October 1903. In the presence of many distinguished people representing both the city and various church denominations, the founder of the YMCA movement, Sir George Williams, formally opened the doors with a handsome silver key. Ever since this prominent landmark towering 110 feet high has stood as a tribute not only to Nonconformity (as Trinity United Reform Church nowadays) but also to the perseverance of the influential Samuel Ryder.

The leaders of the churches in those days displayed wonderful courage in coming to terms with such a big sum as the eventual £11,400 entailed in developing Trinity church. Nevertheless, giving is an essential act of worship and all along the members of the new church showed great generosity. By the close of the opening ceremonies, nearly £7,000 was accounted for leaving an outstanding balance of £4,400 to be found.

The two centres of Congregationalism joined forces in helping to strengthen this aspect of Nonconformity. The Rev. Carson duly became the first minister of the new church whilst exercising overall control at Spicer Street. At around the same time Rev. Carson also had to contend with the extra oversight of the Bricket Wood Mission Chapel and the Redbourn Chapel.

The intention was to use the Spicer Street chapel as a temperance and mission centre. Effectively, the Spicer Street chapel became a centre of evangelistic work with the Rev. A. Barrett in charge. Sunday services and Sunday school activities were augmented by a PSA (Pleasant Sunday Afternoon) Society, a Band of Hope, a drill class and a mothers' meeting.

As soon as the new Trinity church was opened, Samuel attended services there rather than at Spicer Street. He finally severed his regular links with his old church when he gave up being the superintendent of the Sunday school there in 1905. This was much to the regret of many but he considered the strain was too great upon his nerves. He opted for the less demanding office of treasurer to the Trinity minister's stipend fund.

In 1906 the responsibility of four churches had begun to take its toll on Rev. Carson. When called to the ministry of a smaller church at Newcastle-on-Tyne, he readily accepted the opportunity to take on less arduous duties.

Accordingly in 1907 the deacons of Trinity church invited the Reverend Frank Harris Wheeler to take Rev. Carson's place. In his twenties, Rev. Wheeler was entering his first full ministry having been an assistant minister serving the Norwich and Lowestoft area. A kind man with powerful preaching skills, he, too, developed a close understanding with Samuel Ryder that was to have a significant impact on sporting history.

Of vital assistance to the Rev. Wheeler in coping with his tasks at the Trinity Congregational and Spicer Street churches was Samuel Buttenshaw, the accountant and secretary of Ryder and Son. His commitment to the Congregational cause dated back to 1882. He was secretary of the committee dealing with all financial matters for both churches and successively general secretary of the Spicer Street chapel and then Trinity Congregational Church. Throughout he held office as a deacon and acted as the editor of the first magazine for these churches in 1909.

Rev. Wheeler immersed himself in his work and, unlike Rev. Carson, stayed well clear of the political arena. His ministry was a happy one renowned for the clarity of his sermons and his outstanding work in helping Samuel Ryder with the religious education of children. He ensured the growth of various organisations associated with the church to make it the social and spiritual focus for its members. These included Bible classes, a women's meeting, a young people's club, a literature society and a Band of Hope.

With the outbreak of war in 1914, Rev. Wheeler became an army chaplain. He attained the rank of lieutenant colonel and was awarded the Distinguished Service Order. It was hoped that he would return to peacetime St Albans but he decided to go elsewhere to further his career.

In 1922 Samuel resigned from his office as a church deacon. At the age of sixty-four he decided that it was advisable to reduce his responsibilities and to concentrate only on his business and his enthusiasm for the game of golf.

Samuel still frequented Trinity Congregational Church and showed his continued interest in the church with a further act of generosity. Early in 1925 he provided land for tennis between Stanhope Road and Breakspear Avenue. Four tennis courts and a pavilion were duly constructed with an entrance off Camp Road. An enthusiastic tennis club was formed for the sole use of the church members and their friends which lasted until the outbreak of the Second World War.

The manse in Ridgmont Road provided by Samuel Ryder

A still greater favour of Samuel to his church was announced at the meeting of Trinity's deacons in September 1925. Samuel had bought a house in Ridgmont Road and had arranged to have it decorated. Then he presented it to the trustees of the church for use as the manse. In so doing, he wished the house to be a memorial to his great friend, Rev. Carson. Ever since, the house has been the residence of all Trinity's ministers whilst in office.

Marjorie followed her father into serving the Congregational cause. In particular she took regular Sunday school classes and supported the girls circle and the women's meeting.

Sister Joan was similarly enthusiastic and joined the membership of Trinity Congregational Church in 1919. Like her father, she concerned herself with young people, becoming joint superintendent for Sunday school work and president of the Mid-Herts Sunday School Union in 1932.

The activities of Trinity Congregational Church and especially its Sunday school classes developed to such an extent that the erection of additional premises became imperative. Two departments of the Sunday school were obliged to meet in separate places some distance from the church. The women's meeting, the young people's club, the Boy Scouts and the Girl Guides were all suffering through lack of accommodation.

At the church's monthly meeting in October 1922 the Sunday school superintendent pleaded for the provision of more facilities for the fast-growing Sunday school. In March 1923 a committee was appointed to look for a suitable site and to start raising the necessary funds. Initially there was a poor response and the project was put on hold.

Things took a much brighter turn in 1926 and again the church was indebted to Samuel Ryder. The committee originally intended to build on land adjoining the church but found the site not large enough. They then approached Samuel with their problem knowing him to be such a strong advocate of Sunday school education. The outcome was the acquisition of an excellent site in Victoria Street secured at a very nominal cost through the generosity of one of Samuel's businesses, namely the herb specialists, Heath and Heather.

A suite of halls was then constructed in close proximity to the church for a total cost of £8,500. The premises enjoyed a frontage of 100 feet with facilities for four departments of graded Sunday school work.

A great friend of Samuel's and a three-times mayor of St Albans, Arthur Faulkner had already left a bequest of £500 in his will for just such a building. He had been superintendent of Trinity's Sunday school for seventeen years until his death in 1922. With his widow contributing £2,000 in addition, it was only fitting that the building was called the Faulkner Memorial Hall. It opened on 30th June 1927 with Samuel in attendance along with the famous writer of children's hymns, the Rev. Carey Bonner.

Fund-raising for the upkeep of churches has never been easy. Trinity Congregational was no exception. At the January meeting of the church in 1919 the minister proposed that a special thanksgiving effort be made to settle the church debt within the following three years. Samuel Ryder was quick to second the motion. By 1935 the church still had a debt amounting to £1,400. Then providence stepped in and an anonymous donor offered to double any amount the church could raise during the year towards extinguishing this debt. With this incentive for their activities, the debt was liquidated by the end of December. It was often part of Samuel's character to do benevolent deeds quietly and there are those who believe Samuel was the generous benefactor in this case.

Along with Arthur Faulkner, Samuel was instrumental in founding the Mid-Herts Sunday School Union in 1904. This union brought together children from all strands of Nonconformity covering 200 square miles of Mid Hertfordshire. Initially thirty-six Nonconformist schools took part comprising 464 teachers and 3,670 scholars. With the aptly-named Mr. Christian as its secretary, the stated object was the saving of the souls of all the children within the area. By their praise and thanksgiving to God, they would be enlightened to face the world with the best values of personal character.

Samuel became president of the union in 1912, serving for two years. Characteristically, he marked his term of office by presenting a trophy for scripture knowledge which he had made by the famous London firm of silversmiths, Messrs. Mappin and Webb. The trophy took the form of a very

39

The scripture examination prize donated by Samuel Ryder

handsome shield consisting of a fine piece of silver encased in wood. On the face was a figure representing victory, bearing laurel leaves, and on the top was a figure of St Columbo teaching children. It was awarded not to the school turning out the most brilliant individual or to the school with the largest number of passes but to the school with the highest percentage of marks. The thoughtful Samuel realized that the advantage gained by using this criteria was that it would give the small school an equal chance with the large school.

The union's annual report for 1914 recorded the generous subscription of five guineas from the retiring president Samuel Ryder. The report continued in glowing terms with the words: 'We have at last to say 'Goodbye' so far as his office is concerned to one who has served us as president for twice the usual term for which this office lasts. Mr. Ryder has proved a true friend of the union and we shall long remember with gratitude his sympathy and help, as well as his ungrudging personal service to the union during two busy years.'

In many ways Samuel portrayed one of the outstanding pillars of Nonconformity for the area. Continually he supported all the denominations of Nonconformity and often acted as the liaison between them. He backed the activities of the Free Church Council and the Christian Endeavour Union in particular.

Mindful of his family background, he became supportive of a renewed Primitive Methodist movement in St Albans. After a gap of twenty-three years, the Primitive Methodists assembled in 1907 as part of the Luton Circuit. Initially they met for weekly services in a room at Dear's Temperance Hotel in London Road. Interest was created and numbers increased to such a degree that a pastor was appointed during October of that year. When the call went out for a permanent place of worship, the philanthropic Samuel came to their aid. At no charge, he provided a highly desirable site

The Primitive Methodist Chapel in Boundary Road (Hertfordshire Archives & Local Studies ref. NM 5B/11)

to the north of the city. The precise location was on the corner of Boundary Road and Culver Road in an area called Bernard's Heath.

Matters progressed with the construction of a school chapel and a small vestry for the sum of £767 10s. It was no surprise that Samuel's wife Helen was asked to formally open the new premises on 1st July 1909. Samuel, not unexpectedly, took his place as the first trustee. Later Samuel and Helen showed further support for the cause, first by opening a fund-raising bazaar and then by opening extended premises in 1925.

Another organisation to receive Samuel's assistance was the Salvation Army. When it required help to raise funds for a new citadel, Samuel once again dipped into his pocket. The precise figures relating to the donations for this cause are not recorded. However the generosity of all the major contributors was indicated when their names were inscribed on stone tablets ready for the stone-laying ceremony of the new headquarters. Six such tablets were produced including one for Samuel which still can be seen today.

Built at a total cost of £4,200, the completed citadel enjoyed a central position along Victoria Street about 100 yards from the Town Hall. As was usual in those days, a splendid stone-laying ceremony took place on

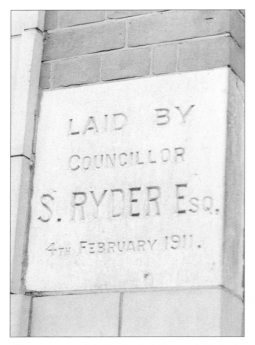

The stone tablet displaying Samuel Ryder's name at the Salvation Army Citadel

The Salvation Army Citadel in Victoria Street

4th February 1911 before a distinguished gathering. Among the speakers was Samuel who praised the Salvation Army for its work for the poor and the homeless in many parts of the world.

At the beginning of the twentieth century the ideals of the Noncon-formists were so closely interwoven with Liberal politics that one always associated the two together. Samuel was a leading figure in carrying the torch for this cause and decided to take a more active role.

4

Civic Duties

S AMUEL HAD witnessed such desperate poverty as a young lad growing up in the Manchester area that he became enthusiastic in support of the underdog long before the days of the welfare state. This great interest in the social welfare of the community led him to fly the flag for the Liberal cause.

The popularity of the Liberal Party at the beginning of the twentieth century was on a high. Membership of the party in St Albans was steadily increasing. New club premises opened up along Hatfield Road in November 1899 and Samuel became a keen member.

His involvement in the affairs of the Liberal Party became ever more time-consuming. Regularly he took the chair at meetings and proved to be a gifted speaker with a keen sense of humour.

Samuel agreed with the view held by many of his fellow citizens that politics ought not to be allowed to enter into municipal life. Nevertheless he felt obliged to serve and proceeded with his candidature for election to the St Albans City Council in 1901. He put up as a Liberal but under the banner of the Progressive ticket along with three fellow Nonconformists. The election proved unsuccessful for Samuel but he was not to be deflected. He persisted with a further election bid in 1903.

On this occasion he ran on what was described as the Liberal and Labour Progressive ticket and again alongside three fellow Nonconformists. Their campaign was greatly enhanced by the loyal support of Rev. Carson and William Bernthal, the new Liberal agent sent from party headquarters. Canvassing was difficult for Samuel as he had been suffering with whooping cough for the previous six months. Consequently he was not able to throw the same amount of vigour into the campaign as he would have done otherwise.

Nevertheless Samuel topped the poll with a record vote of 1,342. On the council he became a member of the Farm and Diseases of Animals Act

The Liberal Club in Hatfield Road

Committee, the General Workers Sub-Committee, the Library Committee, the Urban Authority, the General Purposes Committee and the Clarence Park Recreation Ground and City Improvement Sub-Committee.

However his campaign speeches were criticized by the incumbent mayor (Councillor Slade) at his very first meeting of the full council. Samuel was asked to retract his word 'dishonourable' in describing members of the opposing party, the Moderates. In reply, the Moderates were asked to refrain from referring to the Progressives as 'hooligans'. This wrangling was eventually overcome with the opposing factions becoming so kindly disposed that they indulged in the mutual withdrawal of their accusations.

Samuel's interest in the affairs of the Liberal Party extended to the local parliamentary division. In 1903 he befriended the Liberal candidate Mr. Bamford Slack. It was no surprise that they got on for Slack was a prominent Wesleyan who spoke out for Liberal and women's causes.

William Bernthal was ever resourceful in his role as agent for Mr. Slack. He wrote Liberal words to well-known popular songs and then recruited a Liberal choir from men possessing loud voices. At a suitable moment the choir would burst into song with the aid of placards displaying the necessary words. When asked how the Liberals had managed to assemble such a fine crowd, Samuel quipped, 'Bribery and corruption, St Albans was always noted for it. Anyone would sing anywhere for a few bob!'

In Slack's attempt to unseat the Tory Vicary Gibbs the following year, one heck of a fight developed. Sometimes meetings descended into free fights, stink bombs and rotten eggs thrown through windows. At one meeting Samuel was on the platform when the Liberal's rising star David Lloyd-George addressed the audience. Ugly scenes disrupted the meeting and efforts were made to overturn Lloyd-George's car. The police had their work

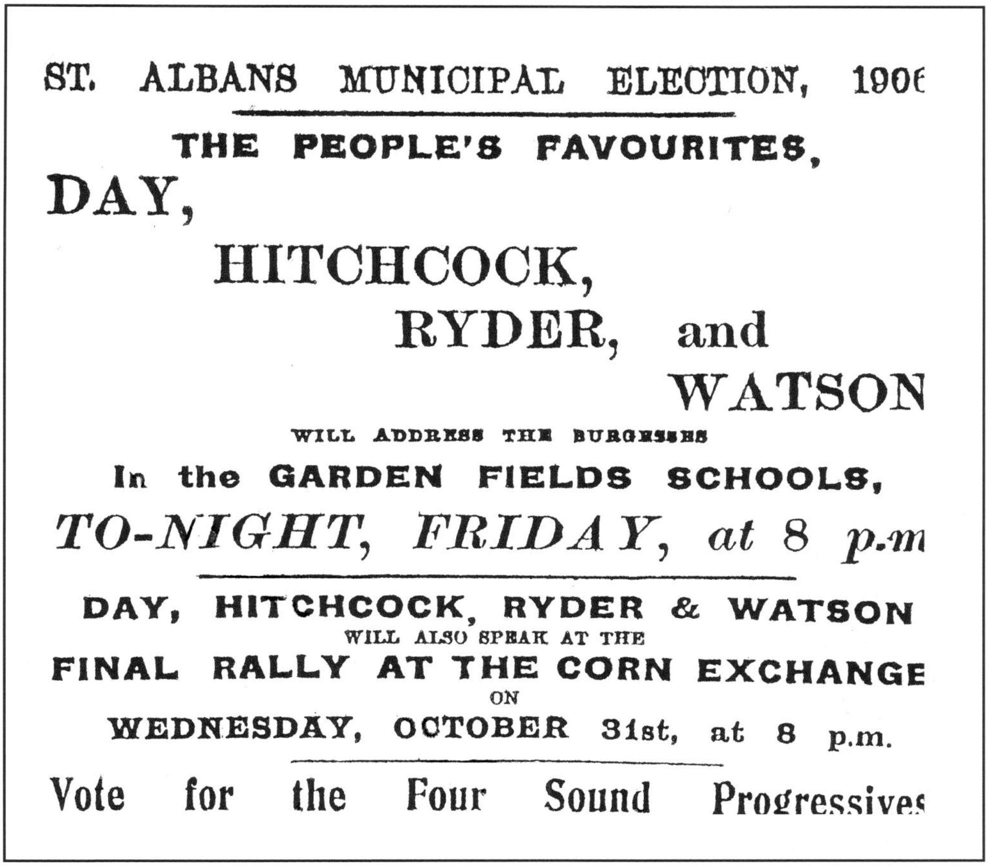

ST. ALBANS MUNICIPAL ELECTION, 1906

THE PEOPLE'S FAVOURITES,

DAY,

HITCHCOCK,

RYDER, and

WATSON

WILL ADDRESS THE BURGESSES

In the GARDEN FIELDS SCHOOLS,

TO-NIGHT, FRIDAY, at 8 p.m

DAY, HITCHCOCK, RYDER & WATSON

WILL ALSO SPEAK AT THE

FINAL RALLY AT THE CORN EXCHANGE

ON

WEDNESDAY, OCTOBER 31st, at 8 p.m.

Vote for the Four Sound Progressives

An election advertisement for the Progressives

cut out to keep order, especially when they escorted Lloyd-George from the hall.

Mr. Slack proved the victor with the slender majority of 132. A triumphant torchlight procession followed with Mr. Slack perched atop a lorry and supported by the Liberal choir. By now they were singing a rendition of 'John Brown's Body' of which the chorus went:-

'Glory, glory, hallelujah
Mr. Slack goes marching on!'

At the following election Winston Churchill, temporarily disillusioned with the Conservatives, spoke as a motivated young Liberal in support of Bamford Slack. Later, back at his home, Samuel remarked to the family 'That young Churchill will go far! What a speaker!' In hindsight surely an understatement. On this occasion Slack was up against Mr. Hildred Carlile representing the Tories but the result was reversed.

Nevertheless the audience derived much joy during the campaign especially from one song put to the tune of 'Dolly Grey'. This time the Liberal choir chorused:-

'Goodbye Carlile you must leave us
Pack your bag and off you go.
We've got Slack to represent us,
It's all arranged you know!
Can't you hear the people shouting?
He's the man for us you see,
Goodbye Carlile you must leave us
Goodbye Mr. C!'

On several occasions subsequently Samuel was asked to stand as a parliamentary candidate for the Liberal Party but each time declined the invitation.

As an influential businessman of the city, Samuel made a very good first impression on the city council. For his second year he had the added responsibility of sitting on the Watch Committee which was accountable for police matters. Little did he reckon on what was to come.

The outcome of the 1905 municipal election secured a Liberal majority on the city council. This cast an aspect of uncertainty over the question of the mayoralty. In the event of the Moderates being in control, Councillor Worssam would have been the likely candidate for mayor. With a Liberal win, Councillor Faulkner was the senior man to have such a claim but the duties of his job in London precluded him from acceptance. It was even deemed possible in some quarters that steps would be taken to obtain the consent of Samuel Ryder to become mayor of the city for the ensuing year. Samuel shrugged off the thought, considering that a councillor should be elected a second time before being asked to accept that position.

It was common practice for the new mayor to be chosen at the 'to be dinner' made up of all the councillors immediately following the annual election. Altogether the names of four senior members of the council were put forward for mayor that year but all of them declined for various reasons. Eventually councillors were unanimous in asking Samuel Ryder to become the city's first citizen expressing his suitability by dint of his diligence with council matters and his tact in running his own business.

Accordingly Samuel became the mayor of St Albans after only two years on the city council. At the age of forty-seven he had the honour to formally represent 17,000 citizens. At the time this was considered a tender age for such an office. In his speech of acceptance, he explained that he was about to speak with great difficulty owing to the fact that he had left his sick bed in order to attend the meeting.

He went on to say that he would endeavour to be strictly impartial as mayor and vowed to represent all political parties and religious creeds. He expressed concern that he found the city £45,000 in debt. Characteristically, he stated his sympathy for the city's poor and resolved to do more for them. Being young he declared that he was not short of audacity and hoped that people would forgive him for having a somewhat incisive

Samuel Ryder – Mayor of St. Albans in 1905-1906

tongue on occasions. In particular he wished to praise the city's officials but he demanded a restructuring in the make-up of the council. He envisaged enlarging the council from sixteen to twenty-four, comprising six aldermen and eighteen councillors. This could be done by dividing the city into wards thereby resulting in cheaper elections.

Following his robing as mayor, Samuel declared to the press that he intended to pursue a policy that would set the city thinking.

It was the custom for the newly-elected mayor to escort the council to his own particular church on the first Sunday after the robing. Usually this was the Abbey or St Peter's. But Samuel broke new ground by taking them to his church, Trinity Congregational in Victoria Street. This almost caused consternation, but the councillors and aldermen thought they'd back up 'Old Ryder' and attended the service officially. Afterwards, several were heard to say it was a beautiful and impressive service, and how surprised they had been!

A short time afterwards Samuel took the chair at the annual banquet of the city council. A large gathering of prominent Hertfordshire men met at the Town Hall to enjoy the excellent catering of Messrs. W. Bugler and Son. Earlier Helen Ryder had tastefully arranged the floral decorations. Vases of

The Town Hall – focus of Samuel's years on the council

fine chrysanthemums and fern fronds adorned the tables while the white covers were concealed by green strands of the smilax vine.

During the speeches that followed, the dean of St Albans remarked on the new mayor's youthful ardour. He hoped that the seeds which the mayor would sow might germinate, flourish and multiply for the benefit of the community.

The local MP, Mr. Bamford Slack, best summed up Samuel's qualities which entitled him to such high office. He described him as a friend for all and an enemy of none. He continued that they all knew he had taken the chair of office because he was inspired to do the best he could not only for the commercial prosperity, but for the social comfort, the domestic contentment and the moral uplifting of the citizens over whom he presided.

Samuel, in turn, spoke of his appreciation in having the support of the citizens. Although he admitted holding some forthright views, he bore no personal bitterness to anyone. Indeed he had enjoyed some humerous moments and he proceeded to give an account of one particular incident. He had received a letter from a gentleman who said he had watched his career from childhood and had predicted a great future for him. His admiration for him had grown as the years went on, and when he heard he had been elevated to that position, he was not at all surprised. When

Samuel turned to the other side of the letter, he found something to the effect that the writer was 'very short' at the present time and could he lend him £5. Amidst laughter, Samuel continued that he did not know what time the post went out but he had not sent that £5 yet.

The following February Samuel was the recipient of a most pleasing tribute which showed the appreciation in which he was held by his own employees. To commemorate his mayoralty, and as a mark of respect, his employees asked him to accept a handsome silver salver complete with an illuminated address. The salver, richly chased, had in its centre a monogram in which were incorporated the initials of Mr. and Mrs. Ryder. The address, designed and made by Mr. E. J. Bryant, of St Peters Street, had, within a conventional border comprised of sweet peas and Canterbury bells, the following inscription:- 'Presented, with a silver salver, to S. Ryder Esq., by his employees on the occasion of his mayoralty of this city as a token of their esteem and very great respect. Signed, on behalf of the contributors, Minnie Spence, Ethel G. Arnold, Alice M. Mallett, Beatrice D. Westell, Augusta Newman, and Rhoda Edwards.' Incorporated into the design were two medallions, one portraying a sower in significance of the mayor's calling, and the other containing a spray of roses.

An endeavour was made to keep Samuel from hearing of the compliment about to be paid him but the secret leaked out, as such secrets do. When he was asked to enter the large workroom of his premises with all his employees arranged in a smiling group around the entrance, his feelings were apparently more of embarrassment than of surprise.

Acting as the representative of the subscribers, Miss Westell said she had been asked by her fellow employees to present to Mr. Ryder a token of their esteem and very great respect. They desired also to recognise the fact that he had been unanimously chosen by the city council to be mayor, of which they were all so proud. They were all proud to think this honour had been conferred upon one whom they thought of as 'His Worship' but they were also happy to think of him as Mr. Ryder, their generous, considerate and kind employer. They felt that the city had never had, nor ever would have, a mayor who had the interests of his employees more closely at heart. Miss Westell concluded by asking the mayor's acceptance of the salver and illuminated address, accompanied by every good wish for himself and Mrs. Ryder and the members of their family.

Samuel, having accepted the gifts, said he knew there was something special going to happen but he had little idea that he was to receive such beautiful presents as these. He had heard from Mrs. Ryder that something was planned and much regretted that she was unable to be present.

49

St. Albans. St. Peter's Street.

St. Peter's Street, St. Albans

However, she had to stay home as their youngest daughter Joan was so very ill. The expressions Miss Westell had so graciously used concerning him, he was sure, were sincere from all of them and he was very grateful that it was so. He would always value these presents and would always think of the givers of them with great pleasure. Miss Westell was so good as to refer to him as a 'master' and he was very glad that the relationship between them was such a pleasant one. He hoped he had done something for his young people. He would always try to do the best he could for them but he could never forget what they had all done for him.

The illness of Joan Ryder was so serious that a specialist was consulted and Samuel had to miss one of the city council's quarterly meetings, but Joan recovered OK.

Samuel was true to his word regarding his concern for the poor. He paid visits to the cottages of the poor in Sopwell Lane and praised the cleanliness therein. He said people should not think ill of these people and promoted a well-attended concert for the unemployed at the County Hall.

The question of housing was one that Samuel had decided views about. He stated that many of the people in the city were not as well housed as his dog was. He accused the Conservatives of going round to some of the poor people and saying that if the Progressives were returned they would be turned out of their houses. But he was unrepentant as ever, and did not mind if the Tories went round and said that 'Ryder was as bad as ever about housing'.

Samuel's idea of dividing the city into wards came up before a formal meeting in April 1906. However, after lengthy discussion, the proposal was defeated by ten votes to five. Once again Samuel was ahead of his time as the division of the city into wards finally became reality in 1913.

Possibly the most contentious issue during his time as mayor concerned the intention to erect telegraph poles in St Peter's Street. As the main thoroughfare in which St Albans' thriving market took place, any major alteration to the scene was bound be the subject of attention. The more so as the street was attractively tree-lined and contained many buildings displaying considerable architectural merit.

A private arrangement between the city council and the Post Office agreed to the erection of telegraph poles on the west side of St Peter's Street. However, as soon as the work started, protests were quickly forth-coming. Many citizens of diverse backgrounds were incensed at the pro-posed disfigurement of their elegant boulevard. A citizens' committee was set up and a petition signed by 199 prominent residents was sent to the postmaster-general.

On behalf of a nervous city council, Samuel Ryder sympathetically listened to the citizens' committee and chaired the subsequent public protest meeting. The uproar had the desired effect. Within weeks the poles had been taken away on the personal orders of the postmaster-general and the wires laid underground. A successful citizens' revolt if ever there was one.

At the beginning of the twentieth century it was customary for the mayor of any English council to carry out the duties of chief magistrate in addition. Samuel gained a reputation of being courteous and exceptionally fair-minded in this regard.

His role as chief magistrate also led to possibly his most embarrassing moment. Thirty-one passive resisters were summoned before the Bench for non-payment of the Poor rate. Amongst those charged at ten shillings was his own wife Helen. Accordingly the mayor had the unique experience of making an order of the court upon his own wife.

Time on the magistrates' bench provided other interesting moments. This was especially true when Arthur Faulkner was on duty with him. Faulkner was an ardent supporter of temperance whereas Samuel appre-ciated a glass of wine with his dinner and a hot whisky toddy at bedtime. So when Samuel prevailed on his fellow magistrates to dismiss a very old gypsy

Frank Salisbury's portrait of Samuel Ryder in mayoral robes

Samuel Ryder's badge as a past mayor of St. Albans

woman without a fine for being drunk and singing in St Peter's Street, Faulkner would not speak to Samuel for a week.

When it came to the annual mayoral banquet during one of Arthur Faulkner's terms of office, the drinks available were decidedly non-alcoholic. Samuel sat with Councillor Hodding who also considered that a meal was incomplete unless accompanied with a good glass of something. Noticing glasses being filled with some yellow drink, Hodding said to Samuel, 'What do you suppose that is, Ryder?' Samuel replied, 'Looks to me like lime juice.' 'My God!' said Mr. Hodding, 'could we get away do you think?' Most timely, the experienced head waiter came with a bottle, filled their glasses and said, 'I think you and Mr. Hodding, sir, will prefer this.' He supplied them with whisky which, at face value, resembled the other drink being served.

The following day everyone, with the exception of Samuel and Mr. Hodding, had been taken ill with stomach trouble. 'Definitely the hand of Providence!', they said. Mr. Hodding added, 'And I imagine that head waiter was no worse off. Saved our lives!'

Others had noticed Samuel's assiduous attention to his magisterial work. This resulted in his appointment to serve on a permanent basis amongst the city's magistrates. He continued to impress and was further honoured in 1914 when he was recommended by the Earl of Clarendon, the then Lord Lieutenant of Hertfordshire, to serve on the more important county bench. He continued in both roles up until the time of his death. Owing to the fact that he suffered from slight deafness, Samuel attended the Bench less often during his final year. This was in the days before magistrates were obliged to retire at seventy years of age.

Samuel remained on the council after his term as mayor, proving victorious on three more occasions at municipal elections. In his time on the city council he served on all its committees except one. Strange to say, he never served on the Finance Committee. That is surprising as he excelled at mathematics at school and developed such a flourishing business. In 1913 he was elevated to the status of alderman. Despite attempts to get him to serve a further term as mayor, he declined the offers. He eventually retired from the council in the autumn of 1916.

In 1911 a special memento of his time as mayor was commissioned. At a council meeting in May of that year the mayor, Councillor Faulkner, raised the question of the desirability of adopting an official badge for the use of ex-mayors of the city on civic occasions. When he attended the Hertford Council's banquet the previous autumn he had noticed that several of the councillors present were wearing these badges. Consequently he made the suggestion that it was time for St Albans to follow this practice adopted by other councils.

Councillor Faulkner duly submitted, for the council's consideration, a badge design that had been prepared by Mr. Robert E. Groves. Mr. Groves was the headmaster of the St Albans School of Art who achieved added recognition as the art designer for the famous St Albans Pageant of 1907. The central feature of the badge's design was a representation of the arms of St Albans in blue enamel and gold, surrounded by suitable ornamentation. It was also proposed that the badges would be produced at the St Albans School of Art, where Mr. J. Polland of Harpenden would work in conjunction with Mr. Groves.

Councillor Faulkner remarked that the badges would not cost the ratepayers anything, as each ex-mayor would pay for his own badge, unless the members of the council were so pleased with his services as to present him with one. Amid laughter, he voiced the opinion that the retiring mayor should have some such memento as this of his year of office. The cost of the badges would be about five guineas but they could be supplied at a cheaper rate in silver gilt no doubt. Then he added, 'But of course we would prefer the real thing.'

Councillor Ekins mockingly responded, 'So would the burglars.' The mayor's proposal was adopted and Samuel duly received his badge displaying his year of office 1905 – 1906.

Once, when questioned about his public life, Samuel replied:- 'Strange as it may appear, I have a strong objection to public life, and always have had. My public work has always been of the nature of a cross. I simply do it from a sense of duty.' The records show he had a sense of pity also.

5

The Marlborough House Years

AS SAMUEL'S SEED business prospered, so the family could afford to move into progressively bigger homes. Initially, when Samuel launched his business in St Albans, the family set up in a modest house on the outskirts of the city. They rented a small semi-detached house at 5 Folly Lane, a mile from the city centre. Four years later, they moved just a few hundred yards to a much larger family house nearer to the city centre. The new home was situated on the corner of Gombard's Street and Worley Road and was then known as 'Scarsdale House'. The position meant convenient access to both Samuel's business and church activities.

In 1906 the family moved once more into a small mansion called 'Marlborough House' off Victoria Street. Samuel took over the mansion from fellow businessman Henry Worssam whom, ironically, later succeeded him as mayor. The house was to be the scene of many events and fond memories.

Marlborough House stood in five acres of grounds complete with a myriad of carefully laid out paths set between well manicured gardens comprising trees, shrubs and an ornamental fountain. A beautiful long drive swept up from Victoria Street past a lodge which guarded the entrance. Behind the tall trees which screened the house from Victoria Street was a 300 yard paddock, a tennis lawn and a croquet lawn. Additionally there was a tradesmen's entrance by way of the gate on Upper Lattimore Road through which passed vehicles accessing the old coach houses and the coachman's cottage.

The brick built mansion comprised accommodation for the family of five, three servants, a dog and a parrot. The family rooms were set around a lovely central wooden staircase complete with two lions carved on the ends of the banisters. When the family managed to get together from their busy lives, they liked to spend time in the morning room or in the conservatory. Samuel had his own room which his daughters referred to as 'dada's study'.

The Ryder family home in Folly Lane

Scarsdale House

Marlborough House

The servants' quarters were in the part of the house facing north. Like other well-off business people the Ryders employed a cook, a housekeeper and a nanny. Unlike some other families, these three staff stayed with the family for many years displaying great loyalty which worked out to the great benefit of all. Nellie Wright was the cook and Evie Siggins the housekeeper. Amy Cook was the much adored nanny usually referred to as 'Cookie'. She had the responsibility of being nurse and maid to Samuel's three daughters, Marjorie, Kathleen and Joan. When any one of the servants went off for their summer holiday fortnight, Helen got into a fearful flap wondering how they'd manage with one short but they coped well enough.

The visit of the family's doctor to Marlborough House combined both business and pleasure. He would arrive in a dogcart with high yellow wheels, driven by a groom, with two beautiful Dalmatian dogs trotting behind. He cut an impressive figure, resplendent as he was in a top hat and attire suitable for visiting Royal Ascot.

After the consultation the bell would be pressed and the maid would bring glasses and a decanter of port. Then Samuel and the doctor would have long discussions over municipal affairs. Samuel, as a keen Liberal, and the doctor, as a dyed-in-the-wool Tory, each strived to convert the other over a glass of port. Inevitably this failed and the doctor would take his leave in

57

School for the Daughters of Gentlemen.

·····························

Pupils prepared for any Examination required. Titled references

———

High School for Girls,

"ROWLATTS" AND "LYNDALE,"

St. Peter's Park, ST. ALBANS.

Principal - - *MISS SHEEHAN.*

(Late Miss Hornsby).

———

Classes for Dancing, Calisthenics and Drawing.

These are open to Children who do not attend the School as Pupils.

·····························

YEARLY, WEEKLY and DAILY BOARDERS RECEIVED.

. . *Prospectus forwarded on application.*

An entry from the St. Albans Almanac of 1900 denoting the school attended by the three Ryder daughters

his dogcart, admired by all the neighbours as he went.

Complimenting his sporting appearance, the doctor was a most skilled surgeon, with a particular concern for children. Parents of St Albans in a crisis would trust a child to his care rather than to any giant of Harley Street.

Setting a precedent for girls of the Ryder families, Samuel's daughters attended the High School for Girls along Hillside Road in St Peter's Park. This became known as the Lyndale School and was run by the sisters, Miss Elizabeth Sheehan and Miss Kate Sheehan, assisted by foreign governors and visiting professors. Samuel naturally took the keenest of interest in the well-being of the school and even donated £500 when he heard of difficulties in its finances.

The girls' education did not end there. At home their parents encouraged reading as an entertainment of lasting pleasure. However their choice of books was rather different. Samuel was relatively unconcerned as to the suitability of any book for his children but Helen strongly disapproved of some.

They were fortunate to have a father who loved reading aloud. He just chose his own favourites as it suited him. Accordingly they were brought up on 'Pilgrim's Progress', 'Sherlock Holmes' and Dickens.

As youngsters they had a complete set of all the first editions of Beatrix Potter. They were thrilled when a new one was published and, in time, like the ones before, it fell to pieces with continual use. The poetry of Hans Christian Andersen made an especially lasting impression on their young minds. His stories were read carefully and quietly, never laughing or crying over them, though they were deeply sorry for 'The Little Mermaid' and for 'The Little Tin Soldier' who melted away into a silver heart.

Other books to intrigue included the pathetic tales of 'Christie's Old Organ' and 'Froggy's Little Brother'. Horror stories also held a strange

Samuel, Marjorie and Helen Ryder outside Marlborough House with chauffeur and Rolls-Royce

fascination but the girls revelled in 'Jack the Giant Killer', 'Blue Beard' and 'Babes in the Wood' despite the accounts of cruelty and tragedy.

Later on there were the books disapproved of by their mother. These were read on the quiet and sometimes under the bedclothes at night. 'Jane Eyre' and 'Wuthering Heights' fell into this category.

When one of the girls protested that a fight in a story was less than fair, their father replied with some sound advice. He said, 'We have never been promised that life would be fair, so never expect it, dear child'.

That was not the only example of Samuel's unique character regarding his sense of fair play and sympathy for the other chap. He could never be persuaded to join in if someone spoke ill of another, always seeing the best in anyone. His daughter Marjorie once came home from a church committee meeting proclaiming, 'You know, dad, if it hadn't been for Mr. So-and-So, we'd have been home hours ago. All his silly questions, I could have shot him!' Samuel calmly said, 'Well, dear, we must make allowances. I know for a fact that his wife feeds him almost entirely on nuts. Now what man can give of his best on such a diet?'

Humour and nonsense were also important elements that constantly provided entertainment in the Ryder household. Samuel was especially amused if people with little sense of humour failed to understand his jokes. On one occasion Samuel was discussing unemployment with an elderly clergyman friend who often came to stay. With a straight face, Samuel told him about a man who had just got a good job cutting holes in Gruyère cheese. The curious clergyman replied, 'I always thought that they were done by machinery, one is always learning!'

Another amusing incident occurred with the same gentleman. Just as the Lord's Prayer was begun prior to breakfast, the telephone rang. The family's parrot, from his cage in the corner, yelled, 'I'll go! I'll go!' An apology was made to the clergyman and Helen placed a cloth over the cage. The parrot didn't take too kindly to that and promptly sang the first line of 'Onward Christian Soldiers!' over and over again in what was described as wobbly soprano. That finished prayers for the morning. When it was suggested moving the cage away next time, the clergyman replied, 'But I like the animals to take part! The Lord God made them all you know!' Sense of humour or not, his heart was in the right place.

Thanks to their parents' foresight, the girls were given the opportunity to appreciate music and drama. From time to time, they would be taken to see the famous personalities appearing on stage or at concerts. It was a great help that some friends owned a box at the Royal Albert Hall. Operas, plays and Shakespeare were all listened to avidly although it was singers of the class of Clara Butt, Dame Melba, Ellen Terry, Henry Irving and John McCormack who were the individual stars. The family's favourite production was 'Charlie's Aunt' for which they knew the jokes and laughed in anticipation of them. Local talent was not neglected for Samuel was responsible for the inauguration of free concerts given by the St Albans Philharmonic Society.

During his mayoral year Samuel commissioned a young artist of his acquaintance, Frank Owen Salisbury, to paint three pictures. Salisbury, a keen Wesleyan, lived nearby at Harpenden and was starting to get established with exhibitions of his works at the Royal Academy. Samuel wished to accelerate his career which, for the most part, was as a portrait painter.

The largest of these pictures was a massive life-size portrait that depicted Samuel standing in his robes as mayor and wearing the mayoral chain. The mace was placed decoratively in the canvas and to the right was artistic lettering which read, 'Samuel Ryder, JP, Mayor of St Albans, 1906.' The original of this painting now hangs proudly in the dining room of the Verulam Golf Club known as the Ryder Room.

The other two paintings which Salisbury produced for Samuel Ryder consisted of family portraits. One was a charming circular portrait of Samuel's three daughters. Joan was then aged two, Kathleen eleven and Marjorie thirteen. The artist's title for the painting was 'Playmates'. The work had a pleasing charm, the colouring being light, principally pearly greys. The third portrait showed Samuel's sister Jenny with her daughter Constance.

Years later Samuel commissioned two more pictures. In 1927 Salisbury painted a fine portrait of Samuel in oils on canvas. Like the other family portraits, the family retain possession of this one as well at the time of writing. Another noted artist of the day, Miles Fletcher de Montmorency, had so im-

The 'Playmates' painting by Frank Owen Salisbury

pressed Samuel with his work that he commissioned him in 1931 to paint an imposing portrait of his famous golf coach Abe Mitchell. It, too, can be found in a room of the Verulam Golf Club known as the Abe Mitchell Lounge.

Much thought went into celebrating the various birthdays of the three girls.

For Marjorie's twenty-first birthday in 1914, the immediate family had a quiet celebration at Marlborough House. However, the following day was marked by a special gathering for 273 partygoers. On this occasion it was decided to conduct the ceremonies at Ryders' business premises on Holywell Hill. The order room was commandeered and transformed into a dining hall complete with bunting, flowers and the flags of the allied countries engaged in the First World War. Karl Kapp's Band provided the music. Amongst the many gifts presented to Marjorie were an elegant diamond and pearl pendant along with a string of seed pearls from her parents.

Two years later it was the turn of her sister Kathleen (known as 'Kitty' within the family) to celebrate her twenty-first. The party took a very different form on this occasion for the horrors of war were never far from everyone's lips at the time. Consequently the garden party at Marlborough House was thrown open to 150 wounded servicemen from the nearby Napsbury War Hospital and the Bricket House Hospital. The band of the Coldstream Guards entertained and food was served from a big marquee.

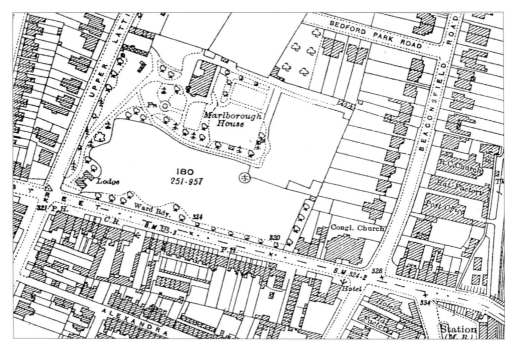

Map of St. Albans showing the Ryder family mansion and the nearby Trinity Congregational Church

From her parents Kathleen received a novel watch pendant, the watch consisting of a small platinum ball heavily encrusted with diamonds and suspended upon a platinum neck chain. Additionally they gave her a handsome platinum and diamond ring.

At this latter event the youngest sister Joan, aged twelve, was a prominent figure among the helpers but sadly the celebrations marking her own twenty-first are not on record.

Generous by nature and generous by deed were certainly qualities rightly attributed to Samuel Ryder. This philanthropic side of him was especially noticed because he would so often lend his home for charitable purposes. In reality he would readily place the grounds of Marlborough House at the disposal of any organisation with which he had sympathy.

Garden fêtes, concerts or meetings were the usual events to attract Samuel's benevolence although his home once played host to a flower show for the St Albans Adult School. Frequently a marquee was erected to provide catering from Messrs. Slaters and stalls were put up as and where necessary. It was a regular feature to construct a platform upon which bands could entertain or speakers eulogise. Songs, sketches and dialogues were performed, occasionally accompanied at the piano by Helen Ryder.

From time to time Marjorie and Kathleen might sing a song or two whilst young Joan could often be found helping to run a stall.

The grounds lent themselves ideally for games and sports. In-itiative was used in providing ac-tivities such as hoop-la, Aunt Sally and cake competitions. A range of sports was set up and proved very popular. Tennis, putting, archery, bowls, croquet, deck quoits, three-legged races, egg and spoon races and even a gymkhana were held at various times. All in all it was intended that there was some-thing to suit everyone.

Unsurprisingly, church organ-isations were often the benefic-iaries. If there was money to raise

Samuel Ryder in the grounds of Marlborough House

for a building extension or to cover a debt, Samuel would be only too happy to provide the venue for a fund-raising event. Christian causes to benefit in this way included the St Albans Tabernacle, the Salvation Army, the YWCA and the St Johns Mission Hall.

Fund-raising for charities linked to the war effort were very much in Samuel's mind. Accordingly he staged garden fêtes which raised hundreds of pounds for the Red Cross, the Bricket House Hospital, the War Supply Depot Fund, the Hertfordshire Prisoner of War Fund and the Silver Thimble Movement For Disabled Sailors.

Marlborough House was also the scene of many Liberal gatherings. Liberal groups which participated included the St Albans Liberal Club, the St Albans Women's Liberal Association and the Mid-Herts Liberal Association.

Samuel's charity work did not end there. Before the introduction of state assistance, a variety of charities was set up by well-meaning citizens of the city to provide for elderly and poor residents. Samuel resolved once more to play his part in helping the poor.

The year after he was mayor he became trustee to the city charity known as Lathbury's and Raynshaw's. Originally two separate charities, this was a legacy of the wills of two prominent citizens. The trustees met to decide (a)

Stortford Lodge

how to distribute £50 annually to the most deserving poor people of certain designated parishes and (b) which poor people should have the right to live in three almshouses in Spicer Street. Five years later Samuel became a trustee to another city charity known as Gawen's charity. Similarly, the trustees had to allocate £40 each year to twenty of the poorest people residing in the Abbey parish. In 1914 Samuel forged links with a third city charity called The Cross Street Prize Fund. When the sale of Cross Street Infant School took place, the resulting net proceeds were used to produce dividends. From these dividends it was the job of the trustees to provide prizes for the new school. Samuel withdrew as a trustee of all charities in 1924 to concentrate on his interests in business and golf.

Two other city causes warrant mention of Samuel's benevolence. For a short while, when mayor, he served as a governor to St Albans Grammar School. Then, when the city's famous pageant of 1907 was enacted, he made an important contribution of £25 towards its cost.

Amid the numerous acts of generosity Samuel was responsible for, it is difficult to single one out. However there is an instance which clearly indicates how well off Samuel had become. In 1912 the trustees of the Church Lands charity approached Samuel for a loan so that they could erect six houses on their land in Catherine Street. This charity then owned

64

fifty-four acres and various properties. Under a scheme of the Charity Commissioners, the proceeds that accrued were given over to the maintenance of St Peter's Church and the poor of the parish. This latter factor may have been decisive for Samuel agreed to a loan of considerable size at £2,500. The sum would be repayable with interest at the rate of £4 per cent per annum within thirty years.

There is also plenty of evidence to indicate Samuel Ryder as being a notable landowner. Already it has been shown how he was in a position to donate land for the Primitive Methodist's church, land for Trinity Congregational's tennis club and a property for Trinity Congregational's manse. A newspaper article from 1919 further proves the point. It featured several properties in Samuel Ryder's name being offered for public auction at The Peahen Hotel. These included shops at 15 Market Place and 19 Victoria Street which had been let. The three private residences on offer were those known as 'Southview' in Grosvenor Road and the two in Avenue Road known as 'Berisal' and 'Dursley'. Altogether it is clear that, at some stage, his finances were extremely healthy and he was shrewd enough to buy at the right time which helped to make him his fortune.

As a senior citizen, Samuel opted for a smaller house in June 1923. The sisters of Loreto College bought Marlborough House to expand their facilities for the secondary education of Catholic girls. In its place Samuel and Helen elected to spend their retirement years in a comfortable family house in Clarence Road. They named it 'Stortford Lodge' after Helen's birthplace at Bishop's Stortford. By this time Samuel had decided on a smaller car and exchanged his Rolls Royce for an Armstrong Siddeley.

6

Addicted to Golf

SAMUEL'S LOVE of sport was an inherent part of his make-up. However the many hours spent in establishing his business had taken him away from his beloved sport of cricket. He still broadly supported sport as an important part of his public life. He sat on the Clarence Park Recreation Ground Committee and personally supported campaigns for new swimming baths at St Albans.

Ironically it was his dubious health that brought him back into the sporting domain in a significant manner. At the age of forty-nine he was seriously affected by the stresses and strains of life. On top of his many other responsibilities, his year as mayor had exhausted him. He was close to a breakdown and his doctors advised him to relax more.

Samuel sought the wise counsel of his minister at Trinity Congregational Church – the Reverend Frank Wheeler. Together they discussed the situation and Wheeler suggested that he should accompany him on to the golf course and get some fresh air.

Accordingly one Monday morning in 1907 they went up to Cunningham Hill where five holes were laid out in a field for golf. There the kindly minister did his best to introduce Samuel into the rudiments of the sport. The fascinated Samuel took to golf immediately and became totally addicted to the game.

Challenges always acted as a spur to Samuel and he resolved to master his new sport. He quickly realized he had the perfect practice area within the grounds of his own home. The paddock ran to 300 yards in length which made it ideal for practising his driving and iron play. A low hedge divided the paddock from the croquet lawn and Samuel arranged to have holes cut into the perimeter of the lawn. Then he proceeded to practice his chip shots over the hedge and learned to putt.

To improve his game he hired local professional John Hill as his coach. Hill came to Marlborough House six days a week, come rain or shine, to further Samuel's aspirations. Sundays were an exception. They were out of bounds and kept strictly for the Sabbath of a devout Christian.

After a year of this intense practice, Samuel felt in a position to apply for membership of the nearby Verulam Golf Club. At the time it was the custom of the club for an applicant to play in a three-ball match with the captain and the secretary. In those days social suitability was the dominating factor over any golfing ability. Membership was very much confined to the professional classes. Clergy, barristers, solicitors, doctors and officers from the services largely made up the membership.

A limited number of businessmen were admitted in addition. Samuel qualified in this respect. He was immediately accepted and paid four guineas for his initial subscription to the Verulam Golf Club.

The Reverend Frank Wheeler – Minister at Trinity Church (Hertfordshire Archives & Local Studies ref. NR4 /24)

Verulam Golf Club derived its name from the ancient Roman colony of Verulamium whose ruined fortifications remain nearby as an important historical site. The club was originally instituted in 1905 as a 9-hole course complete with a wooden hut for a clubhouse. Its situation along London Road was conveniently close to the Great Northern Station and just a mile from Marlborough House.

The club owed its formation to the enthusiasm of four prominent local residents – the Hon. Frederick W. Anson, Dr. Eustace Lipscombe, Mr. George E. Marten and Mr. Ernest A. Phillips. They persuaded fifty gentlemen of the neighbourhood to become founder members subscribing ten guineas each to secure a five year tenancy of the park of Sopwell House. They were also responsible for contracting James Braid to map out the course on seventy acres of arable land. To assist him, he had the services of the greens expert Peter Lees and of Messrs. James Carter & Co., seedsmen well-known for preparing grass seeds suitable for golf courses.

Samuel would never tire of talking about any aspect of the game and liked to recall golfing stories that made his moustache quiver in amusement. One story concerned his association with bank manager George Marten. Marten, as one of the four gentlemen responsible for forming the club in the first place, saw it as his duty to help in some way. Accordingly he was appointed to take care of members' handicaps in the days when it was very much a matter for the individual clubs. However he knew little about golf for his observation was that, as Samuel Ryder was the best golfer in the club, he should be given a handicap of scratch. That proved to be a proud recollection for Samuel and rightly so.

Later a new handicapper revised Samuel's handicap but nevertheless he still allocated Samuel with a handicap of four. He was described as never being a long driver. It was his accurate short game which was his forte. His approach play was very sound with his mashie (5 iron) proving to be his favourite club and, with which, he had been known to hole out with on more than one occasion. Frequently a deadly putter, legend recounted that there was an occasion when he and his partner in a foursome had taken only eighteen putts in the round. Surely a record of some description.

Samuel developed a keen regard for the traditions of the noble game. He became a stickler for the rules and, invariably, made sure he always had a copy of the rules with him whenever he was out on the golf course.

His wife Helen did not always approve of his golfing outfits. She once remonstrated with him for going out to play wearing a pink, woollen hat. Samuel countered, 'They all know me at the club, so it doesn't matter what I wear. And if I go somewhere where they don't know me, it won't matter anyway.'

Apparently Samuel had an imaginary friend who advised him and whom Samuel referred to as 'Old Bill'. Golfers with whom he played and who were unaware of the circumstances were completely mystified by his remarks at first. Samuel would come out with comments like, 'Old Bill says I am improving in my driving' or 'Bill thinks I should swing slower'.

At the Annual General Meeting of the Verulam club in 1908, Samuel was elected to the committee for the first time. That was quite remarkable as he had been a member of the club for less than twelve months.

A special meeting of the Verulam club was called in March of 1909 to decide whether the club members were prepared to sanction the committee to sign a new lease for a further twenty-one years. The Earl of Verulam, as landlord and president, was willing to grant the new lease and, at the same time, provide sufficient land to extend the course into a first-class 18-hole course. This was a welcome change of heart from the Earl who,

The clubhouse of Verulam Golf Club in 1914 (Hertfordshire Archives & Local Studies ref. ACC 1162 NO1692)

originally, had been opposed to the golf club. Open champion James Braid had already visited the course and enthusiastically advised on an extension to 18 holes.

The outcome of the meeting was to go ahead with negotiations for the new lease and the proposed 18-hole course. Additionally a comfortable clubhouse would be erected to replace the wooden hut. The remaining question was how to fund these matters and it was agreed to issue £5 debentures. By the time of the Annual General Meeting of 1910, debentures of over £2,000 had been issued and subscribed. Samuel Ryder headed the list of subscribers with a generous contribution of £200. Not only that, he was widely accredited with persuading several others to take up these debentures.

The new clubhouse and 18-hole course both opened for use in 1910. The course covered an area of 136 acres and measured 6,164 yards (or three-and-a-half miles) with a bogey of 79.

By now the course was maturing into an attractive one set in parkland bounded on the one side by the main railway line and on the other by the River Ver. Views of St Albans Abbey dominated the skyline to the north. The fairways were described as being guarded by every conceivable variety of hazard from natural water and trees to gravel pits and sand bunkers, the

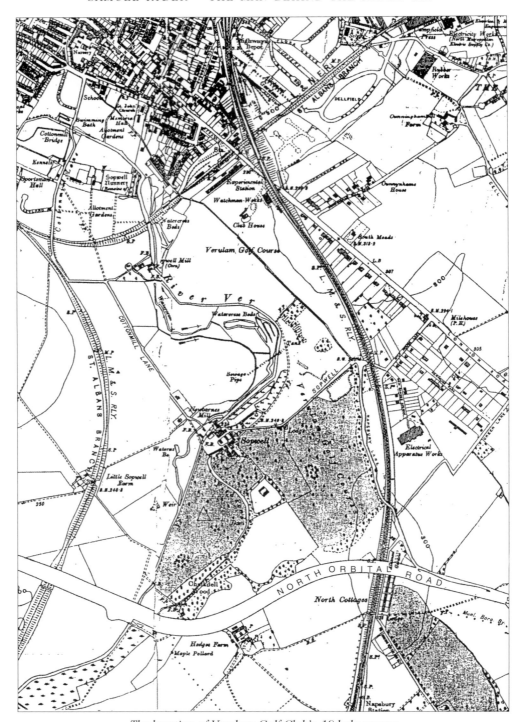

The location of Verulam Golf Club's 18-hole course

latter placed with all the diabolical ingenuity which James Braid could command to trap a pull or a slice. While the indifferent golfer would find it difficult to return a flattering card, the course would rejoice the heart of the player who likes to feel that it 'takes some doing' to put in a good score.

The members of the Verulam club elected Samuel into the office of captain of the club at their Annual General Meeting in 1911. In proposing Samuel for captain, the club chairman, the Hon. Frederick Anson, remarked that he felt certain there was nobody in the club who would fill the office better. He continued that Samuel Ryder had been a very liberal friend to them already, having largely subscribed to

Open Champions James Braid and Harry Vardon who contested the 1912 exhibition match

the debentures, and he believed that rather than let the club get into really impossible difficulties, he would be one of the first to come forward and help them again. Samuel acknowledged his election and said he would do all he could in the interests of the club during the year.

The big event of Samuel's year of office was the formal inauguration of the new 18-hole course which took place on 27th April 1912. This was celebrated with professional golf matches highlighted by an exhibition golf match between the Open champion Harry Vardon (South Herts) and the former champion James Braid (Walton Heath). Braid, of course, had been the architect responsible for laying out the course described as being one of the most diversified in the country in that every hole has characteristics of its own.

These golfing activities attracted widespread interest. Five hundred spectators came from near and far, some by train, some by car and some on foot. Officers of the club were well to the fore including the Earl of Verulam with his wife. Members giving enthusiastic support included Rev. Frank Wheeler and Charles G. Davis.

The arrangements for the match were described as being very complete, thanks largely to the efforts of the officers of the club, aided by their honorary secretary (Mr. K. Atherton Cumming). Mr. G. E. Marten was appointed referee and the umpires were given as Mr. S. Ryder, Mr. A.K. Phillips, Mr. T. H. Robinson and Mr. J.S. Pearson. Mr. A.C. Campbell was in charge of the course and was assisted by a large company of flagmen. Unfortunately a recent spell of dry weather had left the ground hard, making putting especially difficult.

In the morning Vardon and Braid played an 18-hole medal round starting at eleven o'clock. Vardon was round in 74 strokes as against 77 strokes from Braid. Both players had their moments but the main difference between them was the brace of 2s that Vardon obtained at the 15th and the 17th. Vardon's score constituted a new record for the enlarged Verulam course.

```
The approximate scores were:-
Vardon–    Out:  4 5 4 5 4 4 4 4 3 - 37
           In:   4 5 4 4 4 2 6 2 6 - 37    Total 74
Braid–     Out:  4 4 4 5 4 4 5 4 4 - 38
           In:   4 5 4 4 3 4 4 4 7 - 39    Total 77
```

Whilst the match featuring the two champions was in play, the Verulam professional Charles Wallis was having his own private battle with Ernest Penfold from the neighbouring Mid-Herts club. Wallis proved the conclusive winner of this encounter taking 77 strokes to Penfold's 89.

After the morning's medal rounds, there was a break for lunch in a marquee. A splendid meal was served by Messrs. Slaters that satisfied every-one. Leading members of the club and the four professionals then posed for a group photograph before the golfing activities resumed.

The afternoon's golf consisted of a four-ball match with Harry Vardon teaming up with Ernest Penfold and James Braid partnering Charles Wallis. By this time the crowd had grown to well over 600 to witness a close fight in which Vardon and Penfold triumphed by one hole. Penfold was decidedly weak but that did not seem to matter for Vardon created a new course record with his fine individual score of 71. The captain of the club, Samuel Ryder, then took it on himself to generously donate a five guinea prize to the winners. Surely Samuel's first act of financial assistance to the world of professional golf.

The Verulam club staged another exhibition match in 1913. This featured the professionals Tom Ball (Raynes Park) and Charles Wallis (Verulam) against James Bradbeer (Porters Park) and club captain Ernest Phillips who was receiving four strokes (then referred to as bisques). As far as is known, Samuel was merely present on this occasion as an interested spectator. It was to be another ten years before he was to sponsor any more professional golf.

Around this time the question of playing golf on Sundays was probably the biggest talking point in the game and certainly a lively one in St Albans.

On the majority of courses within easy commuting distance of London, Sunday golf was being practised without restriction. A large number of city men, owing to business engagements, had few opportunities of enjoying a full day's play except on Sundays. For many, Sunday was the only day when outdoor recreation could be taken. However in St Albans people were not so tolerant of the situation. There was a very strong feeling of opposition in the district to any Sunday play at all. This came from

An impression of Mr. Samuel Ryder

both members of the club and from residents, both clerical and lay, who condemned any action which diminished the sanctity of the Sabbath. Certainly Samuel Ryder was strongly in the vanguard of this opinion.

This was indeed a most delicate matter which aroused a good deal of controversy at general meetings of the club. It was mentioned how the club had originally been started as a facility for local residents but if the prosperity of the club depended upon attracting members from further afield then their views must be taken into consideration.

It would appear that those wishing for Sunday play succeeded in overcoming the stiff opposition to their demands. A dismayed resident wrote to the local newspaper concerned to see some boys playing hockey around Clarence Park on a Sunday. When he remonstrated with them, he was met with the retort: 'The beggars play golf on Sundays, why shouldn't we play hockey?'. The newspaper concluded that the churches have, so far, been able to make but slight impression on the public with regard to this difficult problem.

At the start of the First World War two rooms in the clubhouse were commandeered by the military authorities. Later on there was a greater concern for it seemed that the military were about to take the club over completely and used it as a camp. In the end that didn't happen but part of

Typical Samuel Ryder

the course known as the Garden Field was taken over for the growing of corn as ordered by the Herts War Agricultural Committee. That entailed the rearrangement of the course which made life difficult. Half of the club members took to the colours and eleven failed to return.

The survival of the club after the war was materially helped by the landlord's continued generosity in reducing the rent and debenture holders waiving their rights to the interest. Samuel was very instrumental in the club's survival not only with his active committee work but in other ways quietly and unobtrusively assisting the club's secretary Joe Pearson in his duties.

The records show that Samuel was on the committee of the Verulam club for well over twenty years. Apart from when he was captain, his time was occupied mostly as the chairman of the Green Committee. He held this position for twenty years and generally received much praise for his efforts. However his long spell in the post was questioned by one member who was heard to remark at a general meeting, 'I understand that the Green Sub-Committee had been appointed for life.'

It was also reported that Samuel had done his dutiful stint at the '19th' by serving on the House Sub-Committee. He couldn't have made too bad a job of that either judging by one captain's comment. At an Annual General Meeting he said, tongue-in-cheek, that he could not remember a bad year when Mr. Ryder was chairman of that particular sub-committee.

In recognition of his many services to the club, the members unanimously elected Samuel as a life member at the Annual General Meeting of 1920.

In proposing the resolution, the chairman said that during the past three years he had known the difficulties and trials of running a club from all points of view as well as the pleasures. He had found that to have a committee of men such as he had had was to make the job simple and exceedingly pleasant. One of the leading spirits of that committee had been Mr. Ryder. Whenever they found themselves faced with a difficulty they had always been able to get the advice and help of Mr. Ryder, who had given it cheerfully. Half the members hardly realised properly what the club owed to Mr. Ryder, and passing this resolution would be only a very small recompense for the work and trouble he had taken right the way through.

Samuel said that it was a great pleasure for him to accept this honour. He had received several honours already but he questioned whether any of them had given him as much pleasure as this one. At the same time he would say that, whatever he had done for the club, he had been amply repaid by the pleasure he derived in playing with the members. They had passed through a stormy time during the war and no one, except those who had been on the committee, knew what they had to go through during that time. One day they had been face to face with the fact that the club was to be closed down because the military were going to take the ground. That should have meant the end of the club, but they had put their heads together and had, in the end, been able to stave that off and had, therefore, been able to save the club. He thanked them all very heartily for the honour they had done him, an honour which he highly esteemed.

In seconding a proposal for captain one year, Samuel made an interesting observation. So many of the mayors elected to serve St Albans were coming from amongst the membership of Verulam Golf Club that it seemed to be more than coincidence. Maybe that was why the 15th hole was given the name 'Mayor's Parlour'. With a mischievous grin Samuel declared, 'They had a very ancient city council and a very wise city council, and when they required a mayor, they looked around the golf club.' By 1930 five club members had served as mayor.

7

Heath and Heather Sponsorship

OR CENTURIES the old Monastery in St Albans was a shrine for the sick and suffering who travelled many miles to frequent its monastic herb garden. The art of healing by herbs was restored to St Albans in 1920 with the start of another major Ryder business. This time it saw the successful combination of the talents of Samuel Ryder and his brother James.

For forty years James Ryder was a schoolmaster in the slums of London, known for his inventive methods of teaching. However, in March 1920, he was forced to retire through ill health. For retirement James had only a meagre pension to fall back on so was very concerned as to his future. He required something that would supplement his income.

That was where he had cause to be grateful for the uncanny insight of his brother Samuel. As they sat down one evening after dinner to discuss matters, Samuel came up with a brilliant suggestion. He reminded James that he had acquired a specialist knowledge of botany. More especially, his hobby had centred on his fascination for the study of herbs and their medicinal value. It had been a lifelong interest and an abiding passion. Why not convert his pastime into a business? Why not utilize his expert knowledge for the benefit of mankind and incidentally for his own?

The erstwhile schoolmaster was persuaded. Samuel advanced some capital although precisely how much is unknown. Matters advanced quickly for James took over a cottage just off Holywell Hill in Albert Street. He then had it suitably converted to provide 980 superficial feet of floor space for use as his herbal establishment. In July 1920 James opened for business.

For a trading name, James ingeniously chose the romantic name of Heath and Heather. The very sound of it suggested the windswept moors and hills, splendid stretches of blue heather and bounding heath. One might rarely get to the moors but by putting at one's disposal a gift labelled as Heath and Heather, the company would succeed in bringing the moors to the purchaser.

James and Alice Ryder who managed Heath & Heather day to day

James set to work diligently. He often could be seen in his shirt sleeves, hammer in hand, nailing up fixtures and putting in long hours of postal work. Along the way he surprised many of his friends by his business acumen, efficiency and enterprise. But the key to his business was his amazing knowledge of the human system and genuine skill in the medicinal value of herbs. In time he was to prove a sincere champion of good health for the greatest number at minimum cost.

At the time the business started, herbalists were not given much credence as scientific men and were viewed with suspicion by many. James undertook a considered campaign to dispel any fears and promote herbalism to a new level of understanding. Within a short time he had convinced many that herbal remedies contained the medicinal qualities to overcome almost every bodily ailment. Even doctors and specialists were seen to procure Heath and Heather products.

The proud claim of the company was that its stock of herbs could help or alleviate all manner of ills. Amongst the range of specific ailments considered suitable for their given remedies were rheumatism, sciatica, troublesome coughs, whooping cough, weeping eczema, headaches, goitre, neuritis, ulcers, influenza, fits, kidney stones, breast abscess, kidney trouble, diabetes, varicose trouble, lumbago, asthma, seasickness and a variety of skin troubles.

The various business premises of Heath & Heather Ltd.

To assist him in the business, James' wife Alice gradually involved herself more and more. As the company expanded, she conducted the day to day management of the staff with the title of the lady superintendent. Furthermore her knowledge increased to such an extent that she regularly gave lectures on herbs and their uses to literary societies and women's institutions.

Of course Samuel was running his own seed merchants' business just around the corner of the street. He was therefore near at hand for wise counsel, developed over many years of extensive business know-how and a unique knowledge of the postal trade. The very name of 'Ryder' associated with the business was a guarantee of the reliable character of the new enterprise.

The early days of the business were not devoid of difficulties. There were obstacles to contend with and overcome. The most obstinate, and the one which threatened to ruin the firm, was a lawsuit. The firm, by its advertisement for Heath and Heather's Herbal Smoking Mixture, recommended a blending of ordinary tobacco with the herbal mixture. Customs took exception to this recommendation as an infringement of the bye-laws affecting the sale of tobacco. The resulting lawsuit turned out to be a blessing in disguise for the press took up the matter sympathetically. Thus Heath and Heather repeatedly came to the notice of the public and it turned into a far-reaching and effective advertising campaign. It all helped Heath and Heather to develop with astonishing rapidity.

Within five years of starting out, Heath and Heather's business expansion had necessitated no less than four removals of its premises. Each time a larger property was required to keep in step with the demand for its products.

A warehouse was acquired at 6 Lower Dagnall Street in March 1922 which provided an extra area of 2,000 superficial feet of floor space. The

A company photograph of Heath & Heather Ltd. from the 1920's

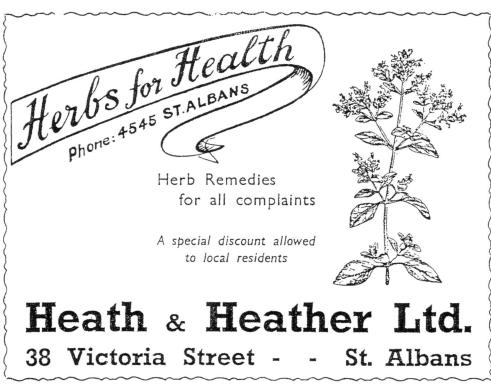

A 1930's advertisement for Heath & Heather

following year James took all of his business to a larger and better equipped building at 53 Victoria Street. Its position meant the premises enjoyed a central location with 8,000 superficial feet of floor space. But still the business grew, until in 1924, the firm transferred to the largest warehouse in the city off Ridgmont Road. The enormous four-storey warehouse with 24,000 superficial feet of floor space had been used as Vyse's hat factory until converted by James for Heath and Heather's use. For his own home, James moved into a detached house at 1 Ridgmont Road which was just yards away from his business.

Over 120 staff had been recruited by this time and businessman Thomas Seaton (later replaced by Alex Simpson) made up the board of directors with James and Samuel Ryder. By demand, the first retail shop selling Heath and Heather goods opened for business on 17th August 1925 at 38 Victoria Street, St Albans. The business grew in such a manner that they could rightly claim theirs was the largest retail firm of herbalists in the world. The proud company motto displayed in their well-known catalogue was always: 'Nothing less than the best'.

Unlike Samuel, James was not actively in the public eye. However he did share sporting interests. He made generous donations to the bowls section of the Camp Liberal Club and, similarly to Samuel, was a keen cricket enthusiast being vice president of St Albans Cricket Club.

Like his brother, James was a keen golfer and also a member of Verulam Golf Club. They both developed an interest in the game that extended to the professional tournaments. They felt a great respect for the skill and calling of golf professionals and considered that professionals in Britain were not treated in a manner that could be called remotely fair. Tournaments were few in number and pay at the clubs was poor. Professionals were not permitted to set foot inside the clubhouse of a golf club. Furthermore the gentry who controlled the clubs looked upon the shabbily-dressed professional as merely a servant of the club whose place was confined solely to the professional's shop.

Accordingly James and Samuel were saddened by the lowly status of the club professional and decided to champion his cause. They would endeavour to go out of their way to try and do the fair thing for professionals which they esteemed as being an honourable, upright and deserving body of men. Therefore they arranged to promote a professional tournament at Verulam Golf Club that would give some meaningful incentive to the players' careers. At the same time, they would sponsor the tournament under the auspices of their firm Heath and Heather Ltd. which would be a further help in advertising the company. In addition they decided to commission a film of the tournament that survives to this day.

The tournament would consist of 36 holes of medal play and invitations were issued to forty-eight of the leading professionals in the country. The event was unique not only to Hertfordshire but in being the first tournament in Britain in which every entrant was paid £5 for playing plus expenses. Each competitor would be the guest of the firm for the day and the hospitality would include lunch, tea, caddie and railway fare. In this way no single professional would have cause for concern that he would be 'out of pocket' even if he failed to make the prize list.

Arthur Havers – winner of the £500 Heath & Heather Tournament

A total prize fund of £500 was put up for what was billed as the first annual Heath and Heather Tournament. The breakdown of the prize money was as follows:- 1st, £50; 2nd, £25; 3rd, £15; the next four competitors to receive £10 each; the following eight £7 10s. each, and the next five, £5 each.

A fine array of the very best golfing talent in the country contested the event. Six former Open champions in the persons of James Braid, George Duncan, Alex Herd, Ted Ray, J. H. Taylor and Harry Vardon were persuaded to compete. Reigning French Open champion James Ockendon and the talented big hitter Abe Mitchell were also in the field. Additionally Arthur Havers was on hand fresh from his victory in the Open Championship at Troon. All in all, the distinguished entry list was proof of the important standing of the event from the professionals' viewpoint.

The tournament took place on 10th July 1923 over a lengthened Verulam course measuring 6,404 yards with a bogey of 77. An overnight storm greatly improved the condition of the course making it ideal for the players.

Home professional Charles Wallis raised hopes of a famous local victory by sharing the best first round score with a 72. However he fell away badly after lunch leaving the established stars to battle it out. Arthur Havers

(Coombe Hill) atoned for an indifferent morning round of 75 by coming in with a brilliant course record of 67. His aggregate of 142 enabled him to edge out James Ockendon (Raynes Park) by a single stroke. It was a magnificent achievement, worthy of a champion, and was attributable largely to some wonderfully accurate iron shots. His one shadow of an error during the round was at the long 16th – 552 yards against the wind – where he mishit his second shot and took 6. Havers' scorecard read:- Out, 3 3 2 5 4 4 4 3 4 = 32; In, 3 4 5 3 4 2 6 3 5 = 35. Total 67.

The leading final scores were:-	1st.Rd.	2nd. Rd.	Total
A. G. Havers (Coombe Hill)	75	67	= 142
J. Ockendon (Raynes Park)	72	71	= 143
S. Wingate (Wearside)	75	69	= 144
Abe Mitchell (North Foreland)	74	70	= 144
J. Braid (Walton Heath)	74	70	= 144
G. Gadd (Roehampton)	74	70	= 144

The prize ceremony was presided over by James Ryder with his wife Alice distributing the prizes to the successful competitors. By his victory, Arthur Havers was carrying off a £50 first prize which was just £25 less than he gained in winning the Open Championship the previous month.

James Ryder considered that the day's competition marked a new era in the history of golf, for he believed it must set an example to be followed in all parts of the country. He further believed that competitions, in which the professionals were insured against monetary loss, would be common in the future. It was an honour to the Verulam club that the first such tournament had taken place there.

Thanks were paid to Samuel and James Ryder for their innovative tournament firstly by club captain (and mayor) Dr. J. W. Cleveland and secondly by Arthur Havers on behalf of the players. J. H. Taylor rounded off the formalities with a tribute and an observation that, in future, overseas golfers would have a far more difficult task in winning the Open Championship than they had in the past.

The following year Samuel and James decided to sponsor a challenge match with two players for whom they were developing a high regard. The brothers arranged for Abe Mitchell from the North Foreland club in Kent and Charles Whitcombe from the Lansdown club near Bath to do battle on 5th June 1924 with 36 holes of match play over the Verulam course. Mitchell was regarded as the greatest match player of the day and always the British favourite most likely to win the Open Championship. He was up

The opponents for the 1924 challenge match (on the left Charles Whitcombe and on the right Abe Mitchell)

against Charles Whitcombe who had just won the *Daily Mail* £1,000 Tournament at Deal and was one of a trio of brothers rapidly making their names in the West Country.

Under leaden skies, Mitchell and Whitcombe set out in their quest for prizes contributed by the Ryder enterprise of Heath and Heather. The weather kept the attendance down for the morning round in which honours ended up all square with both players round in 75. The rain relented in the afternoon encouraging 400 spectators to follow the play. For the second round Mitchell was in impressive form. He was consistently outdriving Whitcombe so that there were occasions when he could take an iron for his second, whereas Whitcombe had to use a wooden club. Winning three holes in a row from the 6th proved decisive and Mitchell eventually ran out the winner by the clear margin of 5 and 3.

After the match, the Verulam club captain, Mr. G. F. Macdonald, warmly thanked Samuel and James Ryder for promoting such an excellent exhibition of golf. He went on to say that they had been provided with another enjoyable day's golf and hoped that there would be others to follow. Former captain Dr. J. W. Cleveland seconded the vote of thanks saying they had been given an opportunity to see two experts play.

Samuel Ryder expressed his delight in staging the match, suggesting they had been watching two potential champions. Whether that would happen or not he did not know, but Heath and Heather were contemplating challenging the Americans who were coming over. If their challenge was issued and accepted, Mitchell and Whitcombe would be asked to be in the English team. Surely an early inkling of what Samuel envisaged in the future. Nevertheless for a firm based in a small English city to consider sponsoring such an international match at the time was remarkable.

James Ryder commented that the object of such a golf match was to spread the fame of the already famous firm of Heath and Heather. He then expressed the hope that both Mitchell and Whitcombe would come again for the Heath and Heather Tournament, which, for that year, was provisionally fixed for September.

Clearly it had been the original intention to make it an annual tournament but no similar event ever took place again. For some reason it would appear that the brothers had a rethink over their sponsorship plans. Possibly the aspirations of the brothers were already changing from an annual tournament for British professionals to one with an international flavour.

The following event again gave clear indications as to future plans for it was promoted in some quarters as 'The Annual Test between the Professionals of Great Britain and America locally subscribed for a large sum'. Other sources described it as 'The International Match' in which the participants were playing for stakes amounting to £1,000. This time the Ryder brothers arranged for George Duncan and Abe Mitchell to represent Great Britain against Walter Hagen and Macdonald Smith representing America. It would have been difficult to select four better known players.

The 'Test' consisted of 72 holes of four-ball match play to be contested over two courses. The first day's play over 36 holes took place on the St George's Hill course in Surrey and the following day saw the final 36 holes played at the Oxhey club in Hertfordshire.

At the time many golfing enthusiasts were disappointed at the standard of play of the top British professionals in comparison with their American counterparts. Americans were starting to make a habit of running off with the Open Championship. The doubters were constantly shouting, 'All is lost.' However the critics were proved wrong on this occasion for Duncan and Mitchell were to prove an immensely powerful combination.

The match teed off at St George's Hill on 10th July 1924 with the famous amateur Harold Hilton officiating as the referee. The Weybridge course,

The photocall preceding the Annual Test of 1924. (Left to right: Walter Hagen; George Duncan; cartoonist Tom Webster; referee Harold Hilton; P. Kelso, ex-manager of Fulham Football Club; Macdonald Smith and Abe Mitchell)

appropriately set amidst beautiful heath and heather, was the choice of the American duo for their 'home' half of the match. In Hilton's estimation, 2,500 spectators turned out to witness a fine match played in very hot conditions tempered by a gentle breeze.

It was quickly evident that Hagen was out of touch and Macdonald Smith proved to be the strong man on the American side. It was not enough however. The British pair went into a useful lead of 3 up after the first 36 holes. Duncan made the difference with a characteristic piece of brilliance in the afternoon round by winning the 11th, 12th and 14th holes scoring 2, 3 and 3 respectively.

The second day's play was staged in front of 3,000 spectators over the more open stretches of the Oxhey course near Watford. The Americans had chances to overhaul the lead. In the morning they failed with several putts from short range. Then, every time in the afternoon when it seemed they must win a hole, Mitchell's putting denied them.

Mitchell and Duncan held out to win by the margin of 4 and 2. The positive result went some way towards restoring British prestige generally and especially pride amongst the followers of professional golf in Britain. For the enterprising Ryder brothers it was a real tonic for all their efforts.

The better ball scores were:-

St. George's Hill – First Round

Duncan and Mitchell –	Out:	4 4 3 3 4 3 4 3 4 – 32
	In:	4 3 4 5 2 5 4 4 5 – 36
	Total	68
Hagen and Macdonald Smith –	Out:	4 4 4 3 4 3 4 3 4 – 33
	In:	4 3 5 4 2 4 5 4 5 – 36
	Total	69

St. George's Hill – Second Round

Duncan and Mitchell	Out:	3 4 2 4 3 4 4 3 5 – 32
	In:	5 2 3 4 3 5 4 4 3 – 33
	Total	65
Hagen and Macdonald Smith	Out:	4 4 2 3 4 4 4 3 4 – 32
	In:	4 3 4 4 4 5 4 4 4 – 36
	Total	68

Aggregates: Duncan and Mitchell 133; Hagen and Macdonald Smith 137.

Oxhey – First Round

Duncan and Mitchell	Out:	4 4 4 4 4 3 4 5 4 – 36
	In:	4 3 4 4 4 3 3 4 4 – 33
	Total	69
Hagen and Macdonald Smith	Out:	4 4 4 4 4 3 4 4 3 – 34
	In:	4 3 4 4 4 3 3 4 5 – 34
	Total	68

Oxhey – Second Round

Duncan and Mitchell	Out:	4 5 4 4 4 3 4 4 4 – 36
	In:	3 3 4 4 4 3 3 – 24
	Total	(16 holes) 60
Hagen and Macdonald Smith	Out:	4 4 4 4 5 3 4 3 4 – 35
	In:	4 3 4 4 4 3 4 – 26
	Total	(16 holes) 61

Samuel and James had every intention of promoting another international match in 1925 but came to the conclusion that it would be advisable to have a preliminary test beforehand. Their idea of such a test consisted of staging a four-ball match over 36 holes between the tried warriors George Duncan and Abe Mitchell against Ernest and Charles Whitcombe. Ernest Whitcombe had proved himself to be the most consistent British player of 1924 with his win in The *News of the World* Tournament and with being the Open Championship runner-up. Charles Whitcombe, of course, had won the 1924 *Daily Mail* event.

Ready for a four-ball match at Verulam. (Left to right: George Duncan; Charles Whitcombe; Ernest Whitcombe and Abe Mitchell)

Back on familiar ground at Verulam Golf Club, the four players assembled on 4th June 1925 for another Heath and Heather promotion with Harold Hilton as the referee. Delightful weather encouraged a good turnout of spectators who included the proven tournament winners Arthur Havers and George Gadd among their number. Messrs. Duncan and Mitchell were far from their best. Duncan had moments of brilliance but Mitchell was having more than his share of wild tee shots. Indeed, he remarked at one point, 'I do not know what can be the matter with me this morning.' The Whitcombes, by sound, reliable golf, managed a famous victory by 2 and 1.

The better ball scores were:-

First Round

Whitcombes	Out:	4 3 4 4 4 4 4 4 4 – 35
	In:	4 5 4 4 4 3 5 3 4 – 36
	Total	71
Duncan and Mitchell	Out:	5 5 3 4 5 3 3 5 4 – 37
	In:	4 4 5 5 4 4 5 2 5 – 38
	Total	75

Second Round

Whitcombes	Out:	4 4 3 4 4 4 4 3 4 – 34
	In:	4 4 3 4 4 4 4 3 – 30
	Total	(17 holes) 64
Duncan and Mitchell	Out:	3 4 3 4 4 4 3 3 3 – 31
	In:	3 5 4 4 4 4 5 3 – 32
	Total (17 holes)	63

Helen Ryder presented the winners with £50 each and the losers with £12 10s. each. Supporting his wife at the prize-giving, Samuel Ryder thanked the club and its hard working secretary Joe Pearson. He said he was very proud of the course and the professionals who had been playing told him they had some of the finest greens in England. He claimed the reason for staging the match was that he and his brother were anxious to encourage the British professionals and to help them regain the Open Championship, which too often had been going to America.

The club captain (Mr. E. T. Wills) said they were very pleased to have staged the match and congratulated the Whitcombe brothers on their victory. George Duncan and Charles Whitcombe, on behalf of the players, then returned thanks and expressed their appreciation of the encouragement given to professional golf by the Ryder brothers.

The Ryder brothers' perception of 'The Annual Test between the Professionals of Great Britain and America' for 1925 took the form of a singles match. They arranged for Abe Mitchell to play Jim Barnes over 36 holes of match play around the Verulam course. It therefore pitched the expert match player that was Mitchell against the newly-crowned Open champion Barnes from America, although a Cornishman by birth. The match took place on 11th July for the substantial prize of 150 guineas courtesy of Heath and Heather. A large crowd had assembled with Harold Hilton in his usual role as the referee.

Mitchell was superb. Often he was driving around the 300-yard mark and, invariably, ahead of Barnes – sometimes only by a few yards, but at other times by up to forty yards. The rest of his game was also in good shape. His method of using a high pitch or a pitch-and-run to the green produced dividends against the low running approach shot favoured by Barnes. Mitchell putted appreciably better than Barnes who missed a number of good opportunities early on.

Mitchell was a healthy 5 up after the first round and went on to win by the conclusive margin of 7 and 6. To beat the new Open champion so comprehensively was a surprise to many and certainly raised Mitchell's

Jim Barnes with Samuel Ryder

The protagonists in the Annual Test of 1925.
(Left: Jim Barnes. Right: Abe Mitchell)

reputation as a match player to a higher plane than ever. Jim Barnes was full of praise for his conqueror declaring, 'I tried my best, but Abe was too good for me. He gave me few chances, and I made far too many slips.'

The approximate scores were:-

		First Round	
Mitchell	Out:	4 5 2 5 4 4 4 4 4 – 36	
	In:	4 4 4 3 3 3 5 3 6 – 35	Total 71
Barnes	Out:	5 4 3 5 4 4 4 5 4 – 38	
	In:	5 4 5 4 4 3 5 3 5 – 38	Total 76
		Second Round	
Mitchell	Out:	4 3 3 5 4 4 4 6 3 – 36	
	In:	3 4 4 – 11	Total (12 holes) 47
Barnes	Out:	4 3 3 5 4 5 4 4 4 – 36	
	In:	3 4 5 – 12	Total (12 holes) 48

The same two protagonists reassembled on the following Wednesday but this time in partnership to oppose Ted Ray (Oxhey) and Archie Compston (North Manchester). For this four-ball match Heath and Heather had been particularly fortunate in obtaining the participation of the first three players in the recent Open Championship, as Ray and Compston had tied for second place just one behind Barnes. Once again a big gallery followed the play with Harold Hilton as the referee.

The match was a real 'thriller', full of magnificent golf. It was won by Barnes and Mitchell with the last stroke on the last hole. They finished one hole to the good after the match had seen fortunes fluctuate and cause the lead to switch from one side to the other and back again. Compston was quite disappointing but the lion-hearted Ray was up to the challenge. Described as the hero of the match, Ray had the best round of the day in the afternoon with a brilliant 66.

He rivalled Mitchell with his feats of long driving. An outstanding effort on Ray's part was at the 9th (315 yards) in the afternoon when he reached the green with his tee shot. Mitchell's most prodigious strokes enabled him to get on the 16th green (500 yards) with a drive and an iron, and, at the 18th (580 yards), with two woods.

The better ball scores were:-

First Round
Barnes and Mitchell	Out:	4 4 3 5 4 4 3 4 4 – 35		
	In:	4 4 5 3 3 2 4 3 4 – 32	Total 67	
Ray and Compston	Out:	4 4 2 4 4 4 3 4 3 – 32		
	In:	4 5 4 4 4 4 4 3 5 – 37	Total 69	

Second Round
Barnes and Mitchell	Out:	4 4 3 5 3 3 4 5 3 – 34		
	In:	4 4 4 3 4 3 4 3 4 – 33	Total 67	
Ray and Compston	Out:	4 3 3 4 3 4 4 4 3 – 32		
	In:	3 3 3 4 4 3 5 3 5 – 33	Total 65	

The final golf event of 1925 sponsored by Heath and Heather had the added interest of being the decider for an important medal. Since 1919 it had been the practice of The Professional Golfers' Association to award the Ryle Memorial Medal to the leading British professional in the Open Championship each year. It commemorated the memory of the late Mr. A. J. Ryle, an enthusiastic supporter of the PGA and also the brother of the late Bishop Ryle, dean of Westminster.

As Ted Ray (Oxhey) and Archie Compston (North Manchester) had tied for second place in the recent Open Championship, it was arranged for them to play off to ascertain the destiny of the Ryle medal. The Ryder brothers got to hear about this and agreed with the Verulam club to stage the event. Harold Hilton took on the role of referee once more and Percy

Another challenge match at Verulam (Left to right: Archie Compston; Ted Ray; Jim Barnes and Abe Mitchell)

Play in progress for the Ryle Memorial Medal. (Harold Hilton leading Ted Ray with Archie Compston following behind)

91

Perrins was on hand to represent the PGA in his capacity as its secretary. As usual, the Verulam secretary Joe Pearson admirably supervised matters with Messrs. Slaters providing the catering.

Despite recent heavy rain, the course was in splendid condition as Compston and Ray set out on 24th October. Both players struggled early on but Ray's magnificent putting saw him 3 up after the first six holes. Then Compston got his game together. He won five of the last six holes of the morning round to go into lunch 2 up. In the afternoon there was a curious incident at the 11th. One of the stewards accidentally trod on Ray's ball, forcing it into the ground, for which Ray appealed to the referee. However, Compston showed his sportsmanship, and perhaps his disregard of the rules, by kicking the ball out of its unplayable lie, with the result that the hole was halved. At the time Compston was 3 up and he then played steadily to run out the winner by 2 and 1.

The approximate scores were:-

First Round

Compston	Out:	5 5 3 5 4 5 4 4 – 39	
	In:	4 4 4 4 2 5 2 5 – 34	Total 73
Ray	Out:	4 3 3 5 4 4 4 4 – 35	
	In:	4 4 4 5 5 3 5 3 6 – 39	Total 74

Second Round

Compston	Out:	4 4 3 5 4 4 4 4 – 36	
	In:	5 4 4 3 4 3 6 3 – 32	Total (17 holes) 68
Ray	Out:	4 4 4 5 4 4 4 6 4 – 39	
	In:	4 4 4 3 4 3 5 3 – 30	Total (17 holes) 69

After the match Samuel expressed his thanks to all at the Verulam club for allowing the match to take place over their course. He remarked on the excellent condition of the course and said they could not have witnessed any better golf in England than they had that day. Specifically, he challenged other business people with a sporting conscience to come forward and follow Heath and Heather's example. In that way we should have a team ready to fight and stem the American invasion.

In reply the club captain (Mr. T. E. Wills) said they were only too glad to have the match there. He thanked the Ryder brothers for all they did for English professional golf. It could only help in raising the standard of tournament golf in England. He concluded by hoping the 'Yankee' invasion would stop so that the Championship would stay in this country permanently.

Matches sponsored by Heath and Heather Ltd

10th July 1923

£500 Heath & Heather Professional Tournament

5th June 1924

Challenge Match: Abe Mitchell v Charles Whitcombe

10/11th July 1924

Annual Test: Duncan/Mitchell v Hagen/Macdonald Smith

4th June 1925

Challenge Match: Duncan/Mitchell v E.R. & C.A. Whitcombe

11th July 1925

Annual Test: Abe Mitchell v Jim Barnes

15th July 1925

Challenge Match: Barnes/Mitchell v Compston/Ray

24th October 1925

Ryle Memorial Medal Match: Archie Compston v Ted Ray

The captain's wife, Mrs. Wills, then handed Compston the Ryle Memorial Medal, with replica, and both competitors received cheques. In returning thanks, Compston, on behalf of his brother professionals, thanked the Ryder brothers for their fine sportsmanship. He also said the professionals appreciated Samuel Ryder's kindness at which point three cheers were given for Samuel Ryder. Ray endorsed Compston's comments saying the Ryder brothers did a great deal for golf and it was greatly appreciated by the professionals.

Samuel Ryder made the important announcement that it was to be the last of the various tournaments that Heath and Heather would sponsor. After seven of the most important professional golf matches ever staged in Britain, the Ryder brothers intended to continue their keen interest in the game but in another guise.

At the following month's Annual General Meeting, thanks were expressed to Samuel and James Ryder for providing the club with some of the finest golf matches in the world. In addition they were thanked for donating £150 to defray the cost of preparing the course for these matches staged in the name of Heath and Heather.

8

Initiating the Ryder Cup

AT THE prize distribution for the Ryle Memorial Medal played at Verulam Golf Club, the news was made public that the Ryder brothers were about to finalize arrangements with Abe Mitchell in order to retain him as their private professional. Their sole object was that, without any club duties to perform, Mitchell would be free to play in all the important tournaments. Additionally he would have as much practice as he liked and get thoroughly fit with the hope of regaining the Open championship and keeping it in Britain. The Ryder brothers saw Mitchell as the man to repel the American invaders who were threatening to dominate the Open Championship.

These arrangements were to alter very quickly. Samuel discussed matters with his brother and strongly indicated that he wished to have the controlling interest in this initiative. James accepted the situation. He then decided that it would be best to leave future golfing aspirations to Samuel completely and withdrew his interest.

Accordingly it was announced formally that Abe Mitchell had been appointed as the private coach to Mr. Samuel Ryder of St Albans. In this guise, the enthusiasm of a St Albans sportsman provided an Englishman with the facilities to devote his whole attention to preparing himself for an endeavour to return the Open Golf Championship to England from American hands. Abe Mitchell accepted a three-year appointment with Samuel Ryder at £500 a year, with £250 expenses, to be his private professional. The agreement became effective from Christmas 1925.

A condition of the appointment stipulated that Mitchell must be prepared to move home and become resident in St Albans. Mitchell responded quickly and set up home with his wife Dora at 19 Cunningham Avenue barely 300 yards from Verulam Golf Club.

Mitchell would be alleviated of worries and be allowed adequate time for preparing and participating in all the big tournaments and challenge

95

Abe Mitchell's house in Cunningham Avenue

matches. He would have a more realistic chance against many Americans who held private posts and could devote plenty of time for practice. If, therefore, Mitchell were able to bring the Open Championship back to England in the succeeding three years, there would be no happier man in the land than Samuel Ryder. It would be the realization of the only recompense Samuel sought in return for all the generous interest he took in the welfare of English professional golf. It must have made many of Mitchell's friends in the game decidedly envious.

Abe Mitchell was regarded by many experts as the finest golfer of his day. He had been a prominent member of the Cantelupe Artisan Club at Forest Row in Sussex where the artisan movement first established a real hold in Britain. Mitchell spent a little time in Canada as a lumberjack where he developed massive forearms and strong hands. Accordingly he established a reputation for hitting colossal wooden club shots, though the great Harry Vardon best described him as having a good blend of strength, elegance and control. Mitchell was also known as a quiet, unassuming character whose health was often doubtful since his experiences as a gunner during the First World War. Nevertheless he had achieved many tournament victories including two wins in the *News of the World* Tournament and it was thought only a matter of time before he would win the Open Championship itself.

Naturally the engagement of Abe Mitchell meant that he would be seen regularly around the Verulam course. Referring to this, at the following Annual General Meeting of the club, the retiring captain (Mr. T. E. Wills) said there was no doubt that, indirectly, Mitchell's regular appearances would be an advantage to the club. He added that arrangements were being made so that the advent of Mitchell would not place Wallis, the club's professional, at any disadvantage. Indeed, an effort would be made to try and make it of great benefit to Wallis, both financially and otherwise.

An extra reason for the appointment was that Ryder and Mitchell had struck up a great rapport from the moment they'd first met. Quite possibly this was helped by a common love of gardening. As a result, catalogues later referred to Abe Mitchell as being a consultant for Ryder and Son in all matters concerning golf courses. Clearly an extra duty that would be beneficial for both men.

Although it was not Samuel's chief purpose to improve his own game, it quite naturally meant that, on occasions, he got to play golf with his private professional. Abe Mitchell later recalled the only time when they were partners in a four-ball competition of the Hertfordshire

Abe Mitchell with Samuel Ryder

Alliance. Samuel had taken four strokes on the first hole and was still not on the green, which Mitchell had reached in two. Samuel proceeded to survey the line of his approach and said to his caddie: 'What should I do here, caddie?' 'Pick up, sir,' was the ready response.

Samuel's holiday base in Dorset then became an important factor in helping to form his golfing aspirations. For many years Samuel had taken his family for their annual summer holiday to the seaside resort of Weymouth. Staying at The Royal Hotel along the main esplanade, the situation was ideal for his daughters to enjoy the sands just a stone's throw away. In addition it was convenient for the family to attend the nearby Gloucester Street Congregational Church where Helen was once called on to open a bazaar.

The usual day for Samuel on holiday started with a drive of five miles out to Came Down Golf Club where he was a country member. Each morning he liked to play 18 holes and sometimes he would be accompanied by the minister of his holiday church. On other occasions he would have as his playing partner the club professional Ernest Whitcombe or Ernest's assistant, initially his brother Charles and later the younger brother Reggie.

After the game Samuel would sample a spot of lunch from Mrs. Bessie Whitcombe, the stewardess and mother to the Whitcombe brothers. Over

The clubhouse of Came Down Golf Club in the late 1920's

the years Samuel developed a great respect for Mrs. Whitcombe. He was especially pleased to be on hand for a surprise birthday party that the club gave her in 1926. Bessie Whitcombe thought she had her seventieth birthday approaching. The club got to hear about it and set about the preparations. Members arranged seventy candles around the club lounge, a lovely cake with 'seventy' on it and a cheque for £70. In the midst of these celebrations, Mrs. Whitcombe remarked quite casually, 'By the way, I've just looked in the family Bible at all the dates and I'm sixty, not seventy!' The members nearly collapsed with laughter but carried on regardless with the party.

Samuel was most impressed by the brilliant play of the Whitcombe brothers. One day he asked Ernest Whitcombe if he ever played in the important golf tournaments. Ernest replied that he rarely did. If he was away, he wasn't paid for those days by the club. 'And', he said, 'I'd probably have to walk there as the travel costs so much. The Americans come over here smartly dressed and backed by wealthy supporters. The Britisher has a poor chance compared to that.' Samuel considered that something vital was required to rouse golf clubs to take a real interest and responsibility in encouraging young professionals of talent like the Whitcombes.

Whilst Abe Mitchell was concentrating on his game, Samuel Ryder continued to question the poor support generally given to British professionals. There were few professional tournaments in the 1920s when sponsorship was a rarity and recession became a way of life. Ernest Whitcombe's depres-

The Whitcombe Brothers (Left to right: Charles, Ernest and Reg)

sing comments that highlighted the British professional as being the poor relation compared to his American counterpart touched a raw nerve with Samuel. He longed for a level playing field on which British golfers could compete on the same terms with the subsidized Americans. After consulting his friends Abe Mitchell and George Duncan, he decided to provide a positive incentive along the lines of the various international matches already staged between Great Britain and the United States of America.

Around the same time, in April 1926, the *PGA Journal* stated that the PGA had been requested to select a team of four British professionals to play against four American professionals selected by Walter Hagen. The prize money would amount to £525 and the match would be contested over 72 holes on consecutive days. The first day's play would consist of 36 holes at St George's Hill followed by 36 holes the next day at Wentworth. Each player was to play each member of the opposing team and the winning number of holes in each match would be counted for the side. The winning team would be that which scored the highest aggregate number of holes during the two days' play and the player who had the greatest number of holes to his credit would receive an extra prize. The article continued that it was hoped to play the match during the week prior to that selected for the qualifying rounds of the Open Championship.

WENTWORTH CLUB, VIRGINIA WATER,
Telephone: EGHAM 100.

INTERNATIONAL PROFESSIONAL GOLF
MATCH.

Great Britain v. United States of America
(Eight a side),
Will take place on June 4th & 5th, 1926.
First Day ... ... 36 HOLES FOURSOMES.
Second Day ... ... 36 HOLES SINGLES.

PRICE OF ADMISSION:

5/- each day; 7/6 for a two-day ticket.
Tickets may be obtained at the Gate, or beforehand, if
desired, on application to the Secretary.
Members of the Club will be admitted free.
Applications for Member's Tickets should be made to the
Secretary, and must be received not later than June 1st.

*An advertisement for the International
Match at Wentworth in 1926*

Prompted by this forthcoming international match, announcements in *The Times* (26 April, 1926) and in *Golf Illustrated* (21st May 1926) confirmed Samuel's intention to formulate an annual competition between the two countries on an official basis. Clearly here was the opportunity Samuel had been looking for so he made the offer to donate a challenge trophy for the transatlantic encounter which was readily accepted. The match would now be played on 4th and 5th June at Wentworth's new East course. The terms of the match rapidly changed in respect of having eight players on each side and dropping the 'holes up' format in favour of match play. On the first day foursomes matches would be played over 36 holes and would be followed the next day with singles matches over 36 holes.

When it came to the actual fixture, a ten-a-side contest was held. The event was officially promoted by the club professional George Duncan and the club secretary Major J. H. Hind under the auspices of The Professional Golfers' Association. Spectators were obliged to pay 5/- for daily admission or 7/6 for both days' play.

Critics of the state of British professional golf viewed the prospects of a British victory in the Wentworth showdown with disdain. How they were made to eat their words! The Great Britain team pulled off an amazing win by 13 points to 1 with one match halved. All five of the foursomes were won by the British side. Out of the ten singles matches played the next day, eight went the way of Great Britain, with Compston the only loser and Ernest Whitcombe securing a half. Some put the American defeat down to a lack of time to acclimatize but the trouncing was certainly a great morale booster for the British team.

Samuel Ryder generously encouraged matters by providing each winner with a £5 prize. However, for Samuel, the occasion meant rather more than just a golf match. He was keen for the players of both sides to mix and foster goodwill between the two countries. With this uppermost in his thoughts, he provided champagne and chicken sandwiches for all the competitors after the match. One can imagine that would have suited Walter Hagen to a tee!

The full results were:-

GREAT BRITAIN		AMERICA	
Foursomes			
A. Mitchell and G. Duncan (9 and 8)	1	J. Barnes and W. Hagen	0
A. Boomer and A. Compston (3 and 2)	1	T. D. Armour and J. Kirkwood	0
G. Gadd and A. G. Havers (3 and 2)	1	A. Watrous and W. Mehlhorn	0
E. Ray and F. Robson (3 and 2)	1	C. Walker and F. McLeod	0
E. R. Whitcombe and H. C. Jolly (3 and 2)	1	E. French and J. Stein	0
Total	5	Total	0
Singles			
A. Mitchell (8 and 7)	1	J. Barnes	0
G. Duncan (6 and 5)	1	W. Hagen	0
A. Boomer (2 and 1)	1	T. D. Armour	0
A. Compston	0	W. Mehlhorn(1 up)	1
G. Gadd (8 and 7)	1	J. Kirkwood	0
E. Ray (6 and 5)	1	A.Watrous	0
F. Robson (5 and 4)	1	C. Walker	0
A. G. Havers (10 and 9)	1	F. McLeod	0
E. R. Whitcombe(halved)	0	E. French	0
H. C. Jolly (3 and 2)	1	J. Stein	0
Total	8	Total	1
Total aggregate	13	Total aggregate	1

It is reckoned generally that the 1926 International Match at Wentworth was considered as not being the first official Ryder Cup match because Walter Hagen himself had hand picked the American side from only those Americans who had travelled across to play in the Open Championship shortly afterwards. The side was not selected by the American PGA so it was considered only a scratch team. Besides, it contained four players born outside the United States.

However the edition of *Golf Illustrated* dated 11th June 1926 made an important statement which made reference to the on-going General Strike affecting Britain. It plainly got confused between the Ryder brothers though that is of comparatively little consequence. The article stated:-

George Duncan   *Walter Hagen*

'Owing to the uncertainty of the situation following the strike, in which it was not known until a few days ago how many Americans would be visiting Great Britain, Mr. J. Ryder decided to withhold for a matter of twelve months the cup which he has offered for annual competition between the professionals of Great Britain and America. Under these circumstances the Wentworth Club provided the British players with gold medals to mark the inauguration of this great international match.'

Golf Illustrated also made the most of the sporting rivalry between the two countries. First of all it threw out a challenge by backing Abe Mitchell against any American playing in the Open Championship for £500-a-side in a contest by match play over 72 holes. This was taken up by the great Walter Hagen who won a high profile match in June 1926 by 2 and 1. The magazine also announced in May 1926 that it was setting up a fund in a concerted effort to raise the necessary money to send several British professionals to compete in an organised campaign to capture the 1927 US Open Championship. It was thought that £3,000 should be the target for this fund.

Appropriately Samuel arranged for Abe Mitchell to play a challenge match in September 1926 at Came Down Golf Club where his idea for the Ryder Cup first crystallized. Mitchell's opponent was Reggie Whitcombe, the youngest of the three talented Whitcombe brothers. Reggie had taken over as the club's professional from his brother Ernest and was fast establishing his reputation, which included a victory in the West of England Championship.

Five hundred spectators turned up in near perfect conditions to watch the Came Down contest and paid 2/6d for the privilege. At the end of the morning round Whitcombe led by one hole, but Mitchell was at his best in the afternoon with an approximate round of 70 to overwhelm Whitcombe and win by 5 and 4. Mitchell received a handsome prize from the club in addition to his fee but sadly neither figure was recorded.

The approximate scores were:-

First Round

Mitchell	Out:	4 5 4 5 3 p 5 5 5
	In:	2 5 4 4 4 4 4 4 4 – 35
Whitcombe	Out:	4 5 5 5 3 4 4 4 5 – 39
	In:	p 5 4 5 4 4 3 4 4

Second Round

Mitchell	Out:	4 5 4 3 3 4 3 4 5 – 35	
	In:	2 4 4 5 4 3 4 4 5 – 35	Total 70
Whitcombe	Out:	5 5 4 5 3 5 3 4 6 – 40	
	In:	3 4 4 5 5 3 4 5 4 – 37	Total 77

Other golf matches at Came Down that autumn were of a less formal nature. Mitchell played three times against Reggie Whitcombe with different amateur partners making up the foursome on each occasion. One match intriguingly put Mitchell and Ryder on opposite sides but unfortunately no record exists of the result. Samuel had such a regard for the Whitcombes but also concern for their finances that he even provided Reggie with the means to obtain a new golfing outfit for the following Open Championship.

The *PGA Journal* of January 1927 reported that, owing to the unfortunate clashing of dates of the British and American Open Championships, the proposed international match would have to be abandoned for that year. Thankfully, the situation proved to be of a temporary nature for February's *PGA Journal* was most enthusiastic for the Ryder Cup fixture arranged for the following June.

The same edition of the *PGA Journal* announced that it was the intention of *Golf Illustrated*'s fund not only to send a team of British professionals to the US Open Championship but also to the international match for the Ryder Cup. Money for a fund of £3,000 was requested earnestly and donations of £100 each from *Golf Illustrated* and Samuel

by Frank Salisbury

by Miles Fletcher de Montmorency

Samuel Ryder — The Donor

Abe Mitchell — The Inspiration

Ryder himself launched the appeal. By the time the fund finally closed, there was still a shortfall of around £300. True to form, Samuel made up the outstanding balance.

At this time it was clearly the opinion of two influential bodies that an actual Ryder Cup match had not yet been held. *Golf Illustrated* of 10th June 1927 emphasised that there was no Ryder Cup in existence when the 1926 International Match at Wentworth was staged. The PGA's own Journal of May 1927 announced that the first official Ryder Cup match would take place on 3rd and 4th June 1927 at Worcester Country Club in Massachusetts. But, before the British PGA team left for America, Samuel arranged for the players to have a get-together at St Albans.

On 17th May Samuel hosted a lunch in the Verulam clubhouse for the members of the team which had been selected by the Great Triumvirate of golf, Messrs. James Braid, J. H. Taylor and Harry Vardon. Of these, Taylor and Vardon, together with Alex Herd, took the trouble to travel to St Albans to wish the team bon voyage and good luck. More importantly, the Ryder Cup players competed in a 36-hole medal competition the next day for £180 in prize money presented by Samuel Ryder.

Regretfully, only seven of the nine selected members of the team were able to play in the competition. Paris-based Aubrey Boomer was to be met

The Ryder Cup

in Cherbourg by the team en route to America and Abe Mitchell was receiving medical attention. Mitchell had been unwell since winning the *Daily Mail* tournament and was awaiting the results of an X-ray examination. Accordingly Verulam professional Charles Wallis was called in to make up a fourth pairing.

Charles Whitcombe gained victory in this Ryder Cup curtain-raiser thanks to fine rounds of 71 and 72. Whitcombe did not have a 2 all day yet never required more than a 5 to hole out. His aggregate of 143 left him five strokes clear of Arthur Havers and Archie Compston who tied for second place.

The full scores were:-

	1st. Rd.	2nd. Rd.	Total
C. A. Whitcombe (Crews Hill)	71	72	= 143
A. G. Havers (Coombe Hill)	76	72	= 148
A. Compston (Unattached)	70	78	= 148
F. Robson (Cooden Beach)	74	77	= 151
E. Ray (Oxhey)	75	77	= 152
G. Gadd (Roehampton)	75	80	= 155
C. Wallis (Verulam)	80	75	= 155
G. Duncan (Hanger Hill)	77	79	= 156

Afterwards Helen Ryder distributed the prizes to the successful competitors. However her much more important duty was to hand over the Ryder Cup to the safe keeping of The Professional Golfers' Association. It was an especially significant moment because it was the first recorded occasion on which the Ryder Cup itself had been seen.

On that momentous occasion, Samuel Ryder, not unnaturally, made a very happy and appropriate speech. He said that the only condition attaching to the trophy was that, as long as it constituted of international matches against the United States, the matches should be decided by four-somes and singles. If for any unforeseen reason these international matches were discontinued, it was entirely at the discretion of the committee of the British PGA to allocate it for any other competition; the trophy was theirs to deal with as they thought best.

George Gadd, in his capacity as chairman, accepted the Ryder Cup on behalf of the PGA. In a few well chosen words, he thanked Samuel Ryder not only for the handsome trophy but for all he did for professional golf. He continued by saying how very greatly the committee appreciated his very valuable and generous gift. The team would spare no effort to see that the

The 1927 British PGA Ryder Cup selection committee – Messrs. J.H. Taylor, James Braid and Harry Vardon

Mrs. Ryder presents the Ryder Cup to George Gadd – the Chairman of the British PGA

trophy was brought back to this country. Cheers were then accorded Mr. and Mrs. Ryder.

The *PGA Journal* of July 1927 stated that the gold cup was valued at 100 guineas and was a real masterpiece of goldsmith's craftsmanship being of a most elegant and artistic design. There was also mention of this magnificent cup in the edition of *Golf Illustrated* dated 20th May 1927 which said it was manufactured by the well-known London firm of Messrs. Mappin and Webb. Samuel Ryder's influence was evident for the trophy was deliberately topped by the figure of a golfer closely resembling Abe Mitchell.

The day before the Ryder Cup team was due to sail, Samuel's private professional Abe Mitchell was obliged to pull out with what was eventually diagnosed as appendicitis. Samuel must have been concerned as to how the side could possibly match the Americans without their natural leader he dubbed the 'Prince of Denmark'. The enforced team change brought in Herbert Jolly (Foxgrove) as the replacement player. The big disappointment of Mitchell's absence brought about hurried consultations which resulted in Ted Ray (Oxhey) being made team captain. Nevertheless Mitchell travelled with Samuel Ryder to see the team set sail from Southampton on the liner Aquitania.

The 1927 British PGA Ryder Cup team seen off by Samuel Ryder

The Ryder Cup team departed on a wave of enthusiasm with *Golf Illustrated* again to the fore. The magazine's editor George A. Philpot, who was the mastermind behind the £3,000 fund, acted as the team manager. Any hopes of victory were quickly dashed when the Americans took control of the match. Largely by superior putting, America won the first Ryder Cup match by 9½ points to 2½ points. Many doubted Ted Ray's tactics in announcing his order of play so early that the American captain Hagen was able to arrange his line-up as it suited him.

It was reported in the *PGA Journal* of July 1927 that Samuel Ryder had handed the trophy over to the committee of the PGA under a deed of gift. Curiously the actual deed of trust for the Ryder Cup was not drawn up until after the first Ryder Cup match.

To make matters legally binding, Samuel engaged his own nephew Tom Anderson-Davis to draw up the necessary documents. Anderson-Davis was the son of Charles G. Davis, Samuel's brother-in-law and general manager of the Ryder and Son business. Working out of 22 St Peter's Street in St Albans, Anderson-Davis was a formidable young attorney who was later to emulate his uncle as both captain and vice president of Verulam Golf Club.

On 25th July 1927 the deed of trust for the Ryder Cup was executed with the donor given as Samuel Ryder and the trustees representing the

Attorney Tom Anderson-Davis

British Professional Golfers' Association given as James Braid, J. H. Taylor and Joshua Taylor. Initially, eleven conditions were specified in the relevant document. One key clause confirmed Samuel's earlier comment that the Ryder Cup was to remain the absolute property of the British PGA wherever it may be. Matches were to be played annually and be of two days' duration, with the foursomes on day one and the singles on day two.

Importantly, the trust deed maintained that the two participant teams would comprise professional golfers representing Great Britain on the one hand and the United States of America on the other. The clause continued that each team would be composed of eight players (or such other number as shall be arranged). Players would be selected solely by their respective associations but there was no restriction on a player's qualification by virtue of birth or residence. This was to prove a serious omission and be a bone of contention over the following few years.

The idea of playing the Ryder Cup match on an annual basis was short-lived. An announcement in April 1928 said that, with the consent of its donor, Samuel Ryder, the next match for the Ryder Cup was postponed until 1929. It was thought advisable to play the event in alternate years with the Walker Cup match for the amateur players of both countries.

Samuel was determined that the Americans arriving for the first Ryder Cup match on British soil in 1929 would be greeted with appropriate courtesy. Accordingly he decided to entertain the players of both sides to lunch on the day following the American team's arrival.

One wonders if Walter Hagen kept the diners waiting as he was sometimes apt to do to opponents in challenge matches. Even Samuel Ryder was known to have suffered Hagen's lack of punctuality. His daughter Joan once reported that if her father went to visit Walter Hagen and was kept waiting, he would send him an abrupt message to 'hurry up' and didn't mind if he got an equally abrupt reply.

Samuel and Joan Ryder off to a Ryder Cup match

Joan accompanied her father to the 1929 Ryder Cup match staged at the Moortown Golf Club near Leeds on 26 and 27 April. Samuel was delighted to watch Abe Mitchell in Ryder Cup action over the predominantly moorland course. Crowds of 10,000 flocked to the course each day despite the rather cold weather that persisted. The spectators were rewarded with a spirited display from a British PGA side which was victorious by 6 points to 4 points with two matches halved. The result was a surprise to many and put down to a combination of the weather and insufficient time to acclimatize by the Americans. Either way it was a real fillip to British golf fans.

Presenting his own trophy to the home side's captain, George Duncan, must have been a great thrill for Samuel. He was also pleased with the upkeep of the course at Moortown so he sent for Abbott, the head greenkeeper, and publicly presented him with a handsome cheque. Shortly afterwards Samuel made a generous donation of £100 to the Ryder Cup Fund.

Arguments as to which year the first official Ryder Cup match took place were still circulating in 1929. *Golf Illustrated* of 3rd May 1929 confirmed that the Ryder Cup match for that year was the second official match between the two countries. It said that it was irritating to the Americans to claim otherwise and does Britain no credit. Besides being an illegal claim, it smacks too much of hook or by crook, that Britain must stand one up in the series overall.

The original trust deed did not provide for qualification by birth. Nevertheless the American PGA decided that their teams for 1927 and 1929 should consist of players that were native-born and resident in America at the time. This meant star performers like Tommy Armour and Jim Barnes were excluded as both were born outside of America. The British PGA side did not operate any such restriction. Much comment on

Samuel Ryder proudly presents his famous cup to George Duncan, captain of the successful home team in 1929

this matter brought about a revised trust deed, dated 8th December 1929, which meant the players of both sides had to be resident in the country they represented and to have been born there. The new trust deed confirmed the matches as being biennial and was witnessed by the same trustees and donor as previously.

Criticism of the trust deed continued in 1931 as it automatically ruled out foreign-based players like Percy Alliss and Aubrey Boomer from inclusion in the British PGA Ryder Cup side. The selected players were entertained to dinner by members of the Nineteenth Club before leaving for America. After the dinner Samuel Ryder (as donor), Charles Whitcombe (as captain) and Fred Pignon (as manager) took time out to voice their views in a radio broadcast to both Britain and America.

Samuel was destined never to witness a Ryder Cup match in America but was full of praise for the country in his broadcast. He said, 'I admire that community immensely, and I know how much they have done for humanity, especially I know how much they have done for golf. The great lesson they have taught us, not only in golf, but in ordinary affairs, is that whatsoever the hand findeth to do, do it with thy might. Certainly, America has done this in golf, teaching us the value of science, thought, and hard work in this

112

Samuel Ryder giving the 1931 British PGA Ryder Cup team a hearty send-off at Waterloo Station

noble game. The great and growing friendship that exists between these two great communities will be strengthened and increased by the visit of our team. I look upon the Royal and Ancient game as being a powerful moral force that influences the best things in humanity. I trust the effect of this match will be to influence a cordial, friendly, and peaceful feeling throughout the whole civilized world.' In a final flourish, he enthusiastically remarked, 'I have done several things in my life for the benefit of my fellow men, but I am certain I have never done a happier thing than this.'

Again the optimism engendered for sending a fine British PGA Ryder Cup side into battle proved to be somewhat misplaced. The 1931 match at Scioto Country Club in Ohio on 26th and 27th June ended decisively in favour of America by 9 points to 3 points. The visitors had to contend with very oppressive heat as well as a magnificent display of golf from the Americans.

For the 1933 match for the Ryder Cup, daughter Joan was again at the side of her father, who was looking rather frail after a bout of illness. Once more Samuel was pleased to be able to attend a match in support of 'his boys' as he affectionately called the combined British and Irish team.

Samuel Ryder standing between the captains of the 1933 Ryder Cup teams — J.H. Taylor on the left and Walter Hagen on the right

The match, which took place over the Southport and Ainsdale course on 26th and 27th June, resulted in a thrilling last hole win for the British PGA side. It provided a source of immense pleasure for Samuel to enjoy the company of the Prince of Wales and, the more so, when the Prince presented the home team's non-playing captain, J. H. Taylor, with the trophy at the end of play.

Afterwards the PGA expressed its thanks to Samuel Ryder for generously relieving the Ryder Cup Fund of expenses. He had made himself personally responsible for the travelling and hotel costs of the sub-committee which included not only those expenses incurred during the match period but also those in connection with all the preliminary visits that the sub-committee had made to Southport.

The 1935 Ryder Cup team, bound for America, was feted with a grand send-off by the Nineteenth Club, just as their predecessors had been four years previously. Over 260 members and guests enjoyed dinner at The Grosvenor House Hotel at which there was a special toast to Samuel Ryder. In reply Samuel expressed confidence in the departing British PGA side and paid tribute to the mother of the three Whitcombe brothers who had all been chosen for the match. Having lost their father at a very young age, Mrs. Whitcombe had performed wonders at bringing them up despite great

OUR RYDER CUP PALADINS

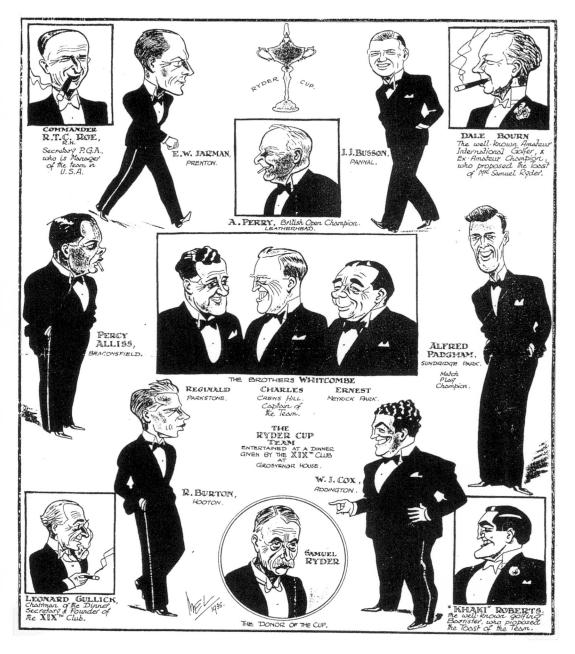

Cartoonist Mel's portrayal of the Great Britain and Ireland 1935 Ryder Cup team at their eve of departure dinner

115

hardship. Their inclusion represented a world golfing record and must have been the crowning achievement of her life.

Interviewed at her Bournemouth home, Mrs. Whitcombe said, 'I do not think we shall win the cup in America until the players get longer practice over there before the match. A week is not long enough.' Her words proved prophetic as the British PGA side tackled the Americans on 28th and 29th September over the tree-lined Ridgewood course at New Jersey. The visitors capitulated to American supremacy by 8 points to 2 points with two matches halved. For a while the British PGA side offered some resistance in the singles until a complete collapse set in over the final nine holes.

Samuel did not live to see another Ryder Cup match but must have been so pleased to have created such a unique golfing occasion. To get together the very best players of the two leading golfing nations at the time and to formulate such a match on an official basis with your own trophy was something very special. The enjoyment, the camaraderie, the excitement, the advancement of the game and the sportsmanship fostered between two great communities are benefits that golfers truly appreciate.

9

Golf Sponsor Extraordinary

WHILST EFFORTS for establishing the Ryder Cup progressed, Samuel continued to play a most active role at his beloved Verulam club. Indeed, the club's Annual General Meeting in 1926 showed just how generous Samuel was in the interests of Verulam Golf Club. A review of the club's accounts for the year revealed that he had made a donation of 100 guineas to show his gratitude of the way in which the club was maintained during the year.

This donation was just one of Samuel's numerous good deeds for the club. In fact, the membership thought so well of him that he was unanimously elected to the captaincy for a second time. His popularity was such that he was elected for the following year as well.

Samuel greeted his acceptance for a second term of office by saying that as they were starting a new chapter in their history, he felt he could really do something for the club. He was referring, in part, to the extension of the clubhouse which had been the culmination of seven years of planning. It had been a disadvantage on their feature days to have a small clubhouse. Shortly they would be able to stage a tournament and provide suitable facilities to match.

The chairman of the meeting disclosed that the key factor in making the clubhouse scheme a success was the very handsome donation of £700 contributed jointly by Samuel and James Ryder. Eventually a total of around £1,800 was required. The architects appointed were Messrs. Mence and Ross and the contractors were Messrs. G. P. Whitby.

The area of the dining-room and smoke-room was doubled, as was the dressing-room accommodation. The ladies' room remained as previously, but there was an addition, in the form of a common room, for the use of both ladies and gentlemen. All of the rooms were comfortably furnished.

The England v Scotland encounter at Verulam Golf Club. Left to right stand Harry Vardon, J.H. Taylor, Samuel Ryder, Sandy Herd and James Braid

Meanwhile the offices were enlarged and the kitchen accommodation increased. A sign of the times that was much appreciated was the installation of electric lighting throughout the premises.

The spacious new clubhouse opened for use during March 1927. Sixty members attended a special dinner in the enlarged dining room to celebrate the completion of the scheme. Samuel presided in the chair and a musical programme rounded off the evening's festivities.

Samuel's financial assistance was again referred to at the club's Annual General Meeting in 1927. It reported that Samuel had given a further £120 for the dressing-room accommodation to be brought up-to-date and had given the club another donation for course preparation work which amounted to £250.

Verulam continued to be the focus of professional golf in the country. Professionals came to play golf with Abe Mitchell but it was the sponsorship of events backed by Samuel Ryder that really put the club on the golfing map.

Back in 1905 Samuel recalled that there had been a famous international match when J. H. Taylor and Harry Vardon representing England took on James Braid and Sandy Herd representing Scotland. At the time these four players were the greatest living masters of the game. Their historic match was for the then substantial sum of £400 decided over four courses – St Andrews, Troon, St Anne's and Deal. Taylor and Vardon carried off the honours for England by 13 and 12.

It occurred to Samuel that the four might like to meet together and fight again. He put it to them and they were keen to do so. It was fixed for the illustrious four to play a 36-hole foursome match over the Verulam course. The game attracted 300 spectators on 14th September 1926. The course was in tip-top condition and arrangements were in the ever reliable hands of Joe Pearson.

The Scots were keen to avenge old scores but had their previous defeat rubbed in instead. Taylor and Vardon quickly established an advantage which they never relinquished. The strength of the English pair was J.H. Taylor who played superbly and putted especially well. Vardon contributed some beautifully played approach shots and the Scottish pair generally were outplayed. Braid, who excelled with his driving, was the better of the two Scots, Herd being below form.

The match finished at the 27th hole where Taylor holed a nine foot putt following an excellent approach by Vardon. This meant that England had prevailed by the conclusive margin of 10 and 9. The remainder of the second round was played out as a four-ball match with Taylor and Vardon again winning, this time by 2 and 1.

Scores:-

Taylor and Vardon	Out: 37	In:	40	Total 77	Out: 34
Braid and Herd	Out: 41	In:	41	Total 82	Out: 39

The following day Samuel Ryder gave a dinner at the Verulam club in honour of the four famous golfers. Samuel presided in the chair, supported on his right by Harry Vardon and J. H. Taylor and on his left by James Braid and Sandy Herd. Speeches and musical accompaniment completed another novel occasion courtesy of Samuel Ryder.

From staging an event for the established old stars, Samuel's next venture was to encourage youngsters to emulate their famous elders. He wished to lay the foundations for raising the standard of ability so that future British players could claim the lost laurels back from their American rivals.

With this end in view, he entertained twelve of the most promising young professionals in the country who had been selected by a committee. The talented young Henry Cotton from the Langley Park Club was invited but, regretfully, had to decline as he was participating in the French Open

The joint winners of the £100 Young Professionals Tournament (On the left Bert Hodson and on the right Jack Smith)

Championship. A 36-hole medal tournament was laid on for the chosen twelve competitors who competed for prize money amounting to £100.

Again the Verulam course was centre stage for the event on 27th September 1927. A morning round of 73 left Bill Twine (Bromley) leading by one stroke from Bert Hodson (Newport) and Fred Taggart (Wilmslow). Twine and Taggart faded away badly in the afternoon. However, Hodson continued his good form with a second round of 73. Jack Smith (Wentworth) followed up his opening round of 77 with the best round of the day when he returned a 70 which enabled him to tie with Hodson for first place.

The full scores:	1st. Rd.	2nd. Rd.	Total
J. A. Smith (Wentworth)	77	70	=147
B. Hodson (Newport)	74	73	=147
W. B. Smith (Hadley Wood)	75	74	=149
R. A. Whitcombe (Came Down)	78	73	=151
W. H. Wooler (Hollingbury Park)	75	78	=153
D. Curtis (Bournemouth)	77	77	=154
J. F. Taggart (Wilmslow)	74	83	=157
A. Easterbrook (Sidmouth)	81	76	=157
W. T. Twine (Bromley)	73	84	=157
W. H. Davies (Prenton)	83	74	=157
J. Donaldson (R. A. C. Epsom)	79	82	=161
C. D. Robinson (Walmer)	83	87	=170

Played concurrently with the young professionals' event was an interesting 36-hole match between the Verulam club professional Charles Wallis and James Bradbeer of Porter's Park. In a game full of good golf, Bradbeer succeeded by 3 and 2.

Helen Ryder presented the winners with their prizes and Samuel then explained his purpose in promoting the tournament for the young professionals. He remarked, 'It is not for me to criticize, but we have discovered that almost every young golfer has a strong objection to practice. That is a very serious thing, because all the trophies of sport are going over to America, and all of us who take an interest in golf want to see something coming to England. Universally among critics of golf it is considered that we are coming back to our own. In the ranks of those who have played here today we believe there are coming champions.' Later his words were proved to be correct for three of the competitors went on to become Ryder Cup players, namely William Davies, Bert Hodson and Reggie Whitcombe. Whitcombe, of course, went one better and won the 1938 Open Championship.

During the following spring, Verulam played host to a contest organised by Samuel between a team of pre-war professionals known as the 'Seniors' and a team of post-war professionals known as the 'Juniors'. Each side consisted of ten players who participated in singles matches over 36 holes on 4th April 1928. Samuel kindly put up 200 guineas as the playing fees and an additional fifty guineas to be divided between the members of the winning team.

On paper, the 'Old Brigade' seemed by far the more formidable combination, but, on the other hand, how would these gentlemen of fifty-plus be able to cope over 36 holes against opponents twenty and even thirty years younger? In any event, the result was a crushing victory for the 'Seniors' who won seven matches, halved two and lost only one.

The 'younger school' were outdriving their rivals in the majority of cases by several yards but the extra lengths they obtained were not sufficient to keep the old men in check. The 'Seniors' seemed to be so infinitely more accurate in their iron play and altogether more reliable in their short game.

Some of the press saw this match as a serious blow for the future of English professional golf. The kindlier ones amongst them reported that the 'Juniors' appeared to be over-awed and dominated by the personalities and fame of their opponents. It would be hardly surprising for their efforts to be clouded with a measure of respect if a youth were drawn to play against a man who was winning championships before he was even born. One 'Junior' said he felt as he used to do at school when summoned to an interview with his schoolmaster.

The contest between the young pretender Henry Cotton and the old warrior J.H. Taylor

Henry Cotton was one who contested every yard of his match against J.H. Taylor. He led the old warrior all the way to the 34th hole where 'J.H.' squared the match by laying a glorious brassie shot stone dead. Then 'J.H.' took the lead at the next with a birdie 2 and sealed the match by also winning the last hole. The only 'Junior' to win was Reggie Whitcombe who beat Sandy Herd by 5 and 3.

The full results were:-

SENIORS			JUNIORS		
J. Bradbeer	(1 up)	1	W. T. Twine		0
F. Robson	(halved)	0	J. Donaldson	(halved)	0
E. Ray	(9 & 8)	1	D. A. Curtis		0
Abe Mitchell	(10 & 9)	1	Jack Smith		0
J. Braid	(5 & 4)	1	R. E. Ballantine		0
J. H. Taylor	(2 up)	1	T. H. Cotton		0
H. Vardon	(4 & 3)	1	B. Hodson		0
A. Herd		0	R. A. Whitcombe	(5 & 3)	1
J. G. Sherlock	(halved)	0	A. J. Lacey	(halved)	0
T. Williamson	(4 & 3)	1	S. Easterbrook		0
Total		7	Total		1

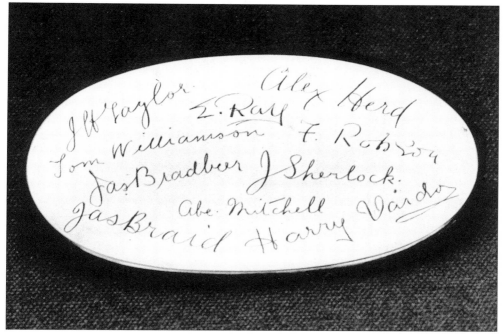

An illustration of Samuel Ryder's special golf bag tag

Following this match, Samuel had a very special memento to accompany him on his rounds of golf. The signatures of the ten famous professionals that made up the 'Seniors' team were expertly embossed on to a silver plated disc. Samuel then used it as a very special tag attached to his golf bag.

In his various efforts to create a home-bred winner of the Open Championship, Samuel devised a special incentive for British players competing at the 1928 Open Championship at Sandwich. He decided to invite the twenty-four British professionals achieving the best aggregate scores to another special tournament at Verulam.

These twenty-four leading players took part in a 72 hole stroke play tournament for prize money amounting to £500 given by Samuel. The competition was regarded as an unofficial British Close Professional Championship and it was intended to make it an annual event.

Many spectators took the opportunity to watch the event on 11th and 12th July but others stayed away, perhaps because of the sweltering conditions. A heat wave had descended in full force and blazing hot sunshine lasted throughout the tournament. Despite copious watering, the hot weather had made the ground hard and players had to contend with some lively bounces making approach shots difficult to judge.

Joint winners of the 'Ryder' British Close Championship (On the left Abe Mitchell and on the right William Davies)

William Davies (Prenton) got off to a flying start by going out in 31 strokes with six 3s. These wonderful figures helped him to rounds of 69 and 73 which led the field after the first day's play. Local favourite Abe Mitchell followed one shot behind in second place with George Gadd (Roehampton) a further stroke behind. Abe Mitchell came to the front after three rounds with a brilliant round of 69 which gave him a lead of three strokes over George Duncan (Wentworth).

With his local knowledge, it was thought that the result was a foregone conclusion for Abe Mitchell. However, William Davies had other ideas and showed that he was not finished with. He set about his final task with grim and courageous determination. The outcome was a card of 71 shots which was great golf under the exhausting conditions. Mitchell could do no better than a 75 which left him tied with Davies at the top of the leader board. Their reward was £75 each.

The leading final aggregates were:

	1st. Rd.	2nd. Rd.	3rd. Rd.	4th. Rd.	Total
Abe Mitchell (Private, St Albans)	74	69	69	75	= 287
W. H. Davies (Prenton)	69	73	74	71	= 287
T. Williamson (Notts)	75	71	71	74	= 291
G. Gadd (Roehampton)	71	73	73	74	= 291
G. Duncan (Wentworth)	77	69	69	77	= 292
T. H. Cotton (Langley Park)	72	75	73	74	= 294
R. A. Whitcombe (Parkstone)	76	75	70	75	= 296

Samuel thanked all those who had been responsible for organising the tournament and congratulated the players on the wonderful performance they had given. In particular he singled out William Davies saying that he was a rising star who had done well in negotiating four rounds of the Verulam course in 287 shots.

Ted Ray, as the senior professional, made it his business to thank Samuel Ryder for his hospitality. He remarked, 'With the encouragement we receive from Mr. Ryder, we have no business in letting Americans take away the trophies like they had. Mr. Ryder is a great supporter of professional golf in this country, so it is up to the younger school to train and be encouraged by tournaments such as these so that they will be able to beat the Americans. Davies and Mitchell have played remarkable golf and I doubt very much whether the Americans could do better than they have done today.'

Ray continued, 'It's when it comes to an Open championship that the Americans are better than the English, for they have the brains.' A dissident voice shouted, 'Rot!' Unperturbed, Ray resumed, 'Golf is seventy-five per cent mental today. Mitchell is one of the finest golfers in the world. There is no American who can hit a ball up to the hole better than he can. When no great interest hangs on the game, British professionals play a better game than their friends across the Atlantic.'

George Duncan added that he hoped there would be fifty players competing in next year's event. He then summed up the general sentiment, 'We are alright amongst ourselves, but we don't want to beat each other, we want to get some young blood to beat America.'

Sadly the 'Ryder' British Close Championship was not to be repeated again. Nevertheless a successful tournament had been held and a glance at the Verulam club's accounts revealed that Samuel had made another handsome contribution of £250 to offset the expenses incurred in staging the professional events of 1928.

An important outcome of the Verulam club's Annual General Meeting of 1929 was the members' unanimous endorsement of a committee proposal to elect Abe Mitchell as an honorary member of the club. It was agreed that his courteous demeanour had endeared him to all the members and that he had done a lot of good work for the club. The Verulam club was largely known because of Abe Mitchell's affliation which had enhanced the club's fame throughout the country. Samuel Ryder observed, 'I tried to get Abe Mitchell here tonight to respond. He has never been heard to make a speech yet and this has frightened him away!'

The same meeting reported on a scheme that was under way to improve facilities at the club. Under this scheme a new shop was being provided for the club professional and the caddie-master. It was also proposed to build a garage, make extra parking available and provide some place for bicycles. The whole cost was estimated at £750 for which Samuel, with typical generosity, put down £100 towards it.

By the grace and inspiration of Samuel Ryder, yet another big golf match took place over the Verulam course on 14th June 1930. On this occasion it transpired to be the third or 'rubber' match between Abe Mitchell and

Leo Diegel

American Leo Diegel. In addition to the agreed stakes, Samuel put up a special prize of £100 for the winner. The hand-bills advertising the event described it as being the deciding test for the professional match play championship. At the time each player was the respective match play champion of his country.

In the first match, held at Moor Park, Diegel eventually won thanks to a heroic forty foot putt at the last after earlier looking as if he were going to win easily. The second match at Blackwell saw Mitchell take his revenge with a comfortably solid victory by 3 and 2.

For the decider, the players had to contend with a blazing hot day described as being almost too hot for golf. They also had to play on a course stretched to some 6,700 yards. However, the effects of sunshine and an east wind made the ground receptive to some phenomenal drives of over 300 yards from both men. Though the greens were immaculate, the wind was strong enough to make the judgement of approach shots very tricky.

From the start Mitchell played with confidence. By lunchtime he was 3 up, having gone round in a superb 70 against 73 from Diegel. Mitchell continued to play great golf in the afternoon and proceeded to a convincing win by 4 and 3. For the fifteen holes played in the second round, Mitchell was three under 4s and without a single 5 to mar his scorecard. By comparison to Mitchell, Diegel's form could only be considered as fair, with little luck on the greens.

One great interest of Samuel Ryder was the study of Shakespeare. Accordingly he was in the habit of visiting Stratford-upon-Avon during the 1920s and 1930s for the season of the Shakespeare Festivals. Along with various members of his family, he stayed at the well-appointed Shakespeare Hotel in Chapel Street. When desired, he attended Stratford-upon-Avon Congregational Church conveniently situated nearby in Rother Street.

The family enjoyed the Shakespeare productions at the old theatre before it was burnt down and at the new Memorial Theatre afterwards. 'Hamlet' and 'Much Ado about Nothing' were ones they often liked to see but

Favourite venues for Samuel Ryder – the old Shakespeare Memorial Theatre (above) and the new Shakespeare Memorial Theatre (below)

The clubhouse of Stratford-on-Avon Golf Club in the 1930's

Samuel's personal favourite character was Falstaff. He always went out just before the scene in 'Henry IV' where the young king snubs his old friend Falstaff in the street. Samuel used to say, 'Young upstart! I'm not going to watch that!' He came back when the scene was safely over.

Through these visits, he got to play golf on the course of the Stratford-on-Avon Golf Club. Right from the first, he took a liking to the place and became a country member. He appreciated spending time in the large club room reminiscent of a baronial hall of some Elizabethan mansion with its massive fireplace and barrel ceiling. There it was the practice for the steward to take him a tray with a bottle of Johnnie Walker whisky and a syphon of soda, compliments of the club.

Samuel was much saddened when the old Memorial Theatre was destroyed by fire on 6th March 1926. When a rebuilding fund was launched for a new theatre, the Stratford club led the way by setting up a Golfers' Fund as part of the necessary fund-raising. Appropriately, club member Mr. S. H. Shakespeare (no relation!) organised a gala week on behalf of the club in July 1927 to raise money for this fund, with the prizewinner of the principal competition receiving the Shakespeare Trophy. Efforts to persuade other clubs up and down the land to run similar fund-raising events brought in a disappointing response and the idea had to be scrapped.

Samuel Ryder opens the new course at Stratford-on-Avon

Samuel started paying visits to the club just after it had moved to a new site at Tiddington Road in 1925. The club had left its old 9-hole course which was set on a difficult clay subsoil, for an 18-hole course with gravel subsoil laid out by the great champion J. H. Taylor. The planting of fir, larch and beech, added to the existing gorse and broom, helped to offset the exceedingly flat nature of the course.

To begin with, the club was content to let the course mature properly and numerous stones were removed. When it was considered as being up to standard, arrangements were put in hand to conduct the official opening of the new 6,200-yard course on 27th April 1928. The captain (Mr. R. Y. T. Kendall) asked Samuel Ryder to drive the first ball with the customary reward of £1 for the caddie who retrieved the ball.

The significance of Samuel being asked to start the proceedings was two-fold. His reputation for initiating the Ryder Cup was spreading but he had also arranged for the opening formalities to be followed by a top class exhibition match. The formidable partnership of George Duncan and Abe Mitchell were to oppose Sandy Herd and Ted Ray in a four-ball competition over 36 holes.

Five hundred spectators turned out to watch the match in beautifully fine weather. However, the players had to contend with a fresh south-easterly wind and fairways made hard by a dry spell. All in all, it was difficult for even the experts to exert much control over the ball.

129

Herd and Ray played the first five holes of the morning round badly and lost them all. They found their form after that, but it did not prevent them from being 5 down at the turn. On the back nine they gained a hole on their opponents to go in to lunch 4 down. Herd and Ray quickly narrowed the margin to only 2 down after a further three holes of the afternoon round. However the loss of those early holes had created too great a deficit to make up and the solid pairing of Duncan and Mitchell ran out the winners by 4 and 2.

Scores:-

Duncan and Mitchell A.M. 68	P. M. 67	Total Aggregate	135
Herd and Ray	A.M. 73	P. M. 68	Total Aggregate	141

The next day the four players changed sides and played another 36 hole exhibition match. This time 700 spectators watched Mitchell and Ray take on Duncan and Herd. Mitchell and Ray were 2 up at the end of the morning round. By the 9th in the afternoon, Duncan and Herd had squared matters and a close battle over the last nine holes resulted in a halved match.

In the evening following this match a dinner was given by the Stratford club in honour of Samuel Ryder and the four visiting professionals. It was held at The Shakespeare Hotel where a lavish meal was enjoyed complete with speeches and musical accompaniment. There was much reference to the immortal bard and several apt quotations amused the diners. Samuel was praised as the great 'impresario' of professional golfers who had brought a star cast to Stratford that weekend.

In reply, Samuel said, 'The members have been very kind to me and have received me as though I am a very great man. Really I am not. My handicap at golf is questionable but my interest in golf is above plus 25.' When he deliberated as to whom he should bring to Stratford to attract the crowds, he decided on the four seasoned veterans, believing their pulling power was as great as any. Playfully he quipped, 'Abe's over forty, though I know he's like me and doesn't look it.'

The club captain, Mr. Kendall, announced that, on the following day, play for the course record would take place between the same four professionals. The club was offering a purse of £25 for the winner which would be handed to Mr. Ryder with the request that he award it the next day. Obviously Mr. Kendall was unaware of Samuel's devout Christian principles for the following day was a Sunday. Accordingly there was no possibility of Samuel being present but he would have been pleased that it was Abe Mitchell who carried off the prize with a course record of 69.

His card read:-

Mitchell Out: 4 3 3 4 4 3 4 4 4-33 In: 3 4 5 3 3 4 4 4 6-36 Total 69

Within a short space of time Samuel was made an honorary member of the Stratford club and later elected both captain and a vice president of the club on 23rd March 1929. This was despite his home base being some seventy miles away in St Albans. A great honour indeed. Also it is interesting to note that it was less than six months since he had completed his second term of captaincy at Verulam Golf Club. Clearly he was in demand.

Samuel stayed on as captain of the Stratford club for the following year as well. He continued to be influential in bringing the top professionals to play at the club. The golf was sometimes more of a social nature with the top local players, both men and women, making up foursomes with the professionals.

A more important fixture for the professionals was another challenge match at Stratford provided by Samuel Ryder on 14th September 1929. This time he put up a prize of £100 for a 36-hole contest with Abe Mitchell and George Duncan opposed to Charles and Ernest Whitcombe. Duncan was obliged to pull out at a late hour and was substituted by another former Open champion in Arthur Havers.

It was the first time that Havers and Mitchell had ever teamed up as golfing partners but it was very effective. Mitchell's driving was exceptional and helped the partnership to cover the first 18 holes in a better-ball score of 63 which put them 2 up. The pair continued to impress and finally got home by 5 and 3.

A year later George Duncan did manage to make his way to Stratford for a challenge match. On 2nd October 1930 he made up a Scotland side with Sandy Herd against England represented by Abe Mitchell and Ted Ray. The result of this encounter was a last hole success for England but the main reason for the visit was a special dinner at The Shakespeare Hotel. Samuel Ryder gave a complimentary dinner in appreciation of George Duncan's successful captaincy of the 1929 British PGA Ryder Cup team. Duncan was delighted at the honour but regretted that 'the chief' was absent. Another bout of ill health meant that Samuel was unable to leave St Albans and had to miss the dinner which he had so carefully arranged.

During one of these visits to Stratford, a professional was invited to a neighbouring hotel on the pretext of seeing the landlord's dog, which was a valuable animal by all accounts. Apparently the professional concerned did not return until the small hours of the morning. Therefore on every subsequent occasion that Samuel Ryder met the said professional, he would humorously recall the circumstances by saying of him: 'Ah, he's a great man on dogs!'

131

The £100 challenge match at Stratford-on-Avon (Standing left to right are Abe Mitchell, Arthur Havers, Charles Whitcombe and Ernest Whitcombe)

Cartoonist sketch of the £100 challenge match

In the 1920s Samuel would often be accompanied by his eldest daughter Marjorie when he was travelling around the world in search of new and interesting plants to introduce into Britain. One special location that they visited was Kirstenboche, the botanical gardens on the slopes of Table Mountain in South Africa. There they discovered a daisy-like flower of brilliant diverse colours growing between the rocky outcrops. On enquiry, they were told it was a common weed called Mesembryanthemum Crinflorium. Samuel was excited for he thought it could be a hardy annual ideally suited for cultivation in Britain. He brought some home and gave it the name 'The Livingstone Daisy' as he

Samuel Ryder on voyage to Africa

thought Dr. David Livingstone must have walked on them during his missionary journeys. To the gratitude of many a gardener, he then proceeded to market successfully his new hardy annual.

This visit was the first of several that Samuel was to make to the African continent. He saw business opportunities for go-ahead young people in a fast developing Southern Rhodesia. Accordingly he bought a farm outside of Umtali for his daughter Marjorie and her husband Leslie Claisen following their wedding in 1929. He paid £4,000 for Matikas Kloof Farm where the new settlers produced cotton, maize and coffee with the help of some government subsidies. Additionally they produced a limited amount of tea and grew seeds to help the Ryder and Son business. Much initiative was needed to make matters profitable. They constructed a dam in the hills for essential irrigation and Marjorie acquired a local medical reputation by attending to sick natives with the assistance of Heath and Heather remedies.

Samuel persuaded his new son-in-law to learn to play golf. Leslie became very keen and, as soon as he settled in Rhodesia, set forth on building a small golf course out of the rough veldt. The greens were produced by the planting of grass root by root followed by watering and rolling by local youngsters.

The scenic setting of Hillside Golf Club in the 1930's

This rough course became the forerunner of the Hillside Golf Club. It enjoyed a most scenic situation set in a valley surrounded by hills and mountains. Some of the mountains formed the densely-wooded jungle known as the Vumba through which ran the border between Rhodesia and Mozambique.

The course was situated in a region known for its farming. The farming fraternity asked Samuel to use his good offices to send a team out from England for a golf match. However a suitable date could not be arrived at for such a match and, in its place, Samuel presented a cup to the Hillside club in July 1933. The cup was inscribed as the Matikas Golf Challenge Cup although more commonly known as the Umtali Ryder Cup. The key factor in this benevolence was that the competition for this trophy would be restricted to registered farmers, their families and dependants playing at the Hillside Golf Club in Umtali.

Back home, the Annual General Meeting of the Verulam club in 1935 accorded the highest possible honour to Samuel when he was enthusiastically elected the club's first vice president. It was recognised that no man had done more to put the Verulam club on the map and if it had not been for Samuel Ryder's substantial help in days gone by, the club might not be in existence. Besides, he had done as much for golf as any man in the country. Deserved praise indeed.

134

10

Goodbye and Thanks

FOR A NUMBER of years it was the custom of Samuel to take his wife and other members of his family to London for Christmas and the New Year. He chose The Langham Hotel in Portland Place. Samuel found it most comfortable and convenient for attending concerts and theatres in the West End.

Samuel had been becoming frail for a year or two when the family travelled to London to spend Christmas in December 1935. On Sunday 29th December, while staying at The Langham, he contracted a chill which developed into pneumonia. His condition worsened and he passed away in the early hours of Thursday 2nd January. His wife and members of his family were with him when he died.

Samuel was laid to rest on the following Saturday at the church he helped to establish thirty-three years earlier – Trinity Congregational in St Albans. The funeral service was conducted by a former minister of that church, the Rev. J. W. McAdam. Afterwards at the graveside, in St Albans' Cemetery, the service was conducted by the incumbent minister, the Rev. W. Morton Barwell, and the Rev. T. W. Hodge of the Hertfordshire Congregational Union.

The family was joined by a congregation representative of the many organisations with which Samuel was associated. The affection in which he was held by his employees was evident by the fact that almost every member of the staff of Ryder and Son (1920) Ltd. and of Heath and Heather Ltd. was present. Golfing tributes were paid by several members of Verulam Golf Club and The Professional Golfers' Association was officially represented by Commander Charles Roe, its secretary. Civic leaders and church elders of St Albans were also prominent amongst those attending.

In recognition of his enduring passion for golf, it was Samuel's wish that his favourite golf club, a mashie, was buried with him. Accordingly his eldest daughter Marjorie made sure it was placed inside his coffin. At the

The late Samuel Ryder   *The grave of Samuel Ryder*

service the coffin was surrounded by 100 beautiful floral tributes and among them was a wreath bearing the inscription, 'With profound sympathy from The Professional Golfers' Association to our vice president and very generous supporter of professional golf.'

As soon as the sad news had reached America, the American PGA responded in kind. Their president, George Jacobus, sent a cable which read, 'Officers and the entire membership of the PGA of America join me in expressing profound grief in loss of one of the greatest figures in golf, Mr. Samuel Ryder, whose name will live for ever in the annals of American professional golf.'

Later glowing tributes were paid to Samuel's service on St Albans City Council and the Bench of St Albans Divisional Sessions. Possibly the most interesting comment came from the former minister of Trinity Congregational Church the Rev. Frank Wheeler. He recalled, 'Much has been said of his interest in sport and in that I can claim a share. I little thought that I was making golfing history when, on a Monday morning long ago, I took him out for the first time on the golf course at Cunningham Hill, and initiated him into the mysteries and intricacies of the sport of which he afterwards became so generous a patron. Surely that should be counted to me for righteousness!'

Joan Ryder in the trial grounds at Roe Hyde

In his will Samuel left an estate of £28,283 gross value. Aside from the immediate family bequests, Samuel had not forgotten his trusted household staff. He left £500 each to his faithful servants Nellie Wright and Evie Siggins and another £250 for Amy Cook who had been both nurse and maid to his three daughters. Two further bequests of £250 each were left to two cousins by the names of Ann and Eliza Dobbins, although where they quite fit into the large family tree is unclear. He did not leave anything to charitable causes because he had already made various donations during his lifetime, calculated to be of greater benefit to all concerned than waiting until after his death.

Brother James died a year later while on holiday in Cornwall. After a relatively uneventful life as a schoolmaster, he had a remarkable career change in which he marketed herbal remedies to great effect. Not only that, for three years he played a notable part with his brother in the sponsorship of British professional golf.

After Samuel's death, his daughter Joan took over the day to day management of Ryder and Son, although Stanley Robinson oversaw matters as the chairman of the company. Business continued to flourish and Ryders' grass seeds were an important factor. An interesting item from their 1939 catalogue read as follows:-

Ryders' former premises as seen on Holywell Hill today

9771 'RYDER CUP' MIXTURE FOR PUTTING GREENS

	1lb.	14lbs.	28lbs.	56lbs.	1cwt.
An ideal mixture, producing a close even turf. It is without Rye Grass.	3/3	40/6	78/-	153/6	302/-

After the Second World War the firm retained its special family individuality when Joan Ryder took over as the chairman. Following a refurbishment of the exhibition hall in 1952, Joan reopened it as the 'Floral Hall' and within it created a model golf green as a display stand. She was particularly pleased in 1954 when she obtained special permission to name a new variety of Ryders' Sweet Pea after Princess Margaret. It was described as being of a beautiful rich rose shade.

In 1948 Joan married Tom Scarfe who was a director of Pamphilon, a local firm that provided house furnishings and house linens. By 1966 Joan had decided to retire and so she sold her interest in Ryders' to R & G Cuthbert. Later Cuthberts themselves were taken over by Suttons Seeds. For her part Joan moved with her husband Tom and their daughter Rosalind to Jevington in Sussex for a well-earned retirement.

The buildings that comprised Ryders' offices and its adjacent exhibition hall were taken over by the Post Office under a council lease. The Post

Office used the buildings for both its administrative offices and for its sorting office until late 1992. The premises were then boarded up to await re-development.

The important one acre site situated in St Albans city centre then became a source of much speculation. Eventually the St Albans City Council devised an innovative development competition and invited architects to put forward plans and financial proposals for the site. A vital consideration was the fact that both of the main buildings were adjudged to be listed buildings.

The major part of the development consisted of housing in an area renamed the Ryder Seed Mews to perpetuate the Ryder name. The accommodation comprised twenty-six properties ranging from one and two bedroom apartments to three and four bedroom townhouses. The theme for golfing names continued with the developers calling the apartments either 'The Birkdale' or 'The Moortown' and the houses 'The Wentworth', 'The Muirfield' or 'The Belfry'. The old exhibition hall was enhanced extensively along the lines of its original appearance with creamed walls and tinted glass windows. The building reopened as a fashionable bar and restaurant known as the Cafe Rouge. The former administrative offices of Ryders' at 27 Holywell Hill were completely stripped internally and converted into a sixty bedroom hotel called the Comfort Hotel. By early 1999 all the work was completed and the hotel and cafe had opened for business. Hopefully Samuel Ryder would have approved.

Joan Ryder also took over as the governing director of Heath and Heather Ltd. on the death of her uncle James Ryder. Other family members became involved with the running of the company. Samuel Ryder's son-in-law Leslie Claisen returned from Rhodesia and joined the board of directors alongside Sydney Mayes, a son-in-law of James Ryder. For a short while James' son Leonard Ryder acted as the company secretary. The faithful Ryder servants Nellie Wright and Evie Siggins changed roles and helped to run a local shop of Heath and Heather for a time.

It was thought that the large warehouse of Heath and Heather in Ridgmont Road might be vulnerable as a bombing target in wartime St Albans. Accordingly the company moved to temporary accommodation at Calverton House near the Cricketers Public House. When they moved back after the Second World War, the remarkable Joan was in the unique position of being the chairman of two public companies at the same time.

By 1946 Heath and Heather had expanded so much that they controlled forty-six shops nationwide as well as supplying other health food retailers and chemists. In 1968 Heath and Heather Ltd. was sold to Associated

Joan Ryder in the board room of Heath & Heather Ltd

Health Foods and various changes of ownership followed. Nevertheless some products bearing the Heath and Heather brand name can still be found under the company name Holland and Barrett, whose headquarters are based in Samuel Ryder House at Nuneaton in Warwickshire.

Joan Ryder must have been an exceptionally busy lady. Despite her business schedule during the week, she always found time for Trinity Congregational Church on a Sunday. In 1936 she pioneered the formation of a junior church to look after youngsters of families attending the morning service. After the death of the other joint Sunday school super-intendent in 1951, Joan took over the duties in her own right. She developed a special reputation for organising popular carol services every Christmas in which the music was mainly provided by the children.

Joan never missed attending a Ryder Cup match in Britain. On her one and only visit to America for a Ryder Cup match in 1983, she was thrilled to visit the home of golf legend Jack Nicklaus. There she delighted the great man by presenting him with a tankard originally given to her father on his birthday by a group of Samuel's golfing friends at the Verulam club.

Helen Ryder died in 1955, aged ninety-one, having outlived her famous husband by almost twenty years. Right up until her death she attended many of the business meetings of the two Ryder companies. Like Samuel, very charitable in outlook, she was an enthusiastic supporter of the Royal National Lifeboat Institution. She was also keenly interested in all ex-service movements and many of them benefitted when she decided to give legacies under her will. However she sent the cheques off in 1952 so that, while still alive, she could enjoy the pleasure of knowing that the causes had been helped.

On the golfing front it was announced on 13th March 1936 that Abe Mitchell was to become 'the Playing Professional' to the Verulam Golf Club. The report continued that the appointment will in no way affect Charles Wallis, the club's professional, who will carry out his duties as usual. Sadly that was not quite

Verulam Club Professional – Abe Mitchell

accurate for poor Wallis had been away from the club for the previous six months owing to illness. In fact Wallis died the very next day and Abe Mitchell was persuaded to succeed him as the club professional. Mitchell remained in post until his premature death at the age of sixty in 1947.

Fate, luck, run of the ball, call it what you like, decreed that Samuel Ryder was not destined to see his great ambition fulfilled – that of Abe Mitchell winning the Open Championship. Five times Mitchell finished in the top six places with a best position of fourth. Mitchell succeeded in winning practically everything else including three *News of the World* titles. As a match player, he obtained an enviable reputation as a world beater and won four and lost two of his matches for the Ryder Cup. Mitchell's standing in the game was honoured when he was made PGA captain in 1934.

Not surprisingly, the Verulam club retains some very interesting reminders of its golden era apart from its fine pictures of Samuel Ryder and Abe Mitchell. Memorabilia includes three hickory golf clubs belonging to Abe Mitchell, Samuel Ryder's own Forgan putter in a plain wooden cabinet and an Abe Mitchell scorecard signed by Samuel Ryder. Any visitor is quickly reminded of the club's golfing heritage as 'The Home of the Ryder Cup' is emblazoned on the marble plaques flanking the main entrance. Additionally the club keeps a replica of the Ryder Cup and a copy of the

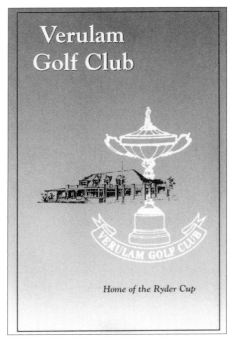

The unique cover of a Verulam scorecard   *Samuel Ryder with his famous cup*

deed of trust relating to the international matches. Interesting photographs that decorate the walls feature the 1923 Heath and Heather Tournament and meetings of the Hertfordshire Alliance from the 1920s. The most important photograph shows Samuel Ryder as captain proudly clutching the Ryder Cup.

Samuel Ryder's name is perpetuated today in three tournaments staged at the Verulam club. There is a club members competition for the Ryder Trophy and an open competition for scratch pairs who compete for the Samuel Ryder Trophy. Professionals from across the region also contest an annual 36-hole PGA event called the Ryder Classic.

The second Ryder Cup for farmers in the former Southern Rhodesia was played on a sporadic basis until 1972. Then African Distillers became aware that there was a distinct lack of national events for farmers and decided to sponsor a golf tournament incorporating the original Umtali Ryder Cup. Only registered farmers, their wives and their dependants were allowed to play in the four-ball-better-ball stableford. The sponsors renamed the event as The *Oude Meester* Tournament after their own brand of liqueur brandy. The tournament always took place at the Hillside Golf Club over two successive days. There were three principal trophies to play for – all with replicas – plus many other prizes. The first 18 holes were for a Ryder

RYDER CUP
OUDE MEESTER SHIELD
RYDER SHOOTING STICK

TOURNAMENT

AFRICAN DISTILLERS LIMITED

Shooting Stick which was deliberate to typify Samuel Ryder. The second 18 holes were for the *Oude Meester* Shield and the Ryder Cup itself was for the 36-hole winners. In today's Zimbabwe this popular event lives on as the Farmers' Ryder Cup.

The deed of trust for the original Ryder Cup twice more required alterations after PGA meetings. From 1961 it was agreed to reduce the matches from 36 holes to 18 holes which allowed for both a morning and an afternoon session and doubled the number of points at stake. Later another meeting brought about the introduction of four-ball matches from **1963**

The 1977 match resulted in not only another American victory but also rumblings of discontent at the regularity of American successes. Jack Nicklaus was instrumental in proposing change to make the event more competitive. Negotiations followed and the way was prepared for a major change in the status quo. Players from Continental Europe became eligible to join their colleagues from Britain and Ireland to make up a united Europe team. Whether Samuel would have approved of the introduction of Continental players is difficult to say. Certainly there are Ryder descendants who are convinced that Samuel would have resisted change, but who can say for sure?

Initially the change to a Europe team did not materially affect the match result. But subsequently the matches have become extremely close-fought encounters with either side likely to prove victorious. The matches now attract huge interest on both sides of the Atlantic. The sheer magic, tradition and history of the Ryder Cup have provided such great competition that just to get on the team is a lifetime's ambition for many professionals. Unlike some other top sporting events, the pride of playing for one's country is sufficient incentive without an extra cash bonus riding on the occasion. The spirit of the Ryder Cup still harbours that great bond of sporting rivalry and friendship that makes the occasion unique. A fitting tribute to the memory of Samuel Ryder.

The engraved gold plate replica prize which was given to the winner of the Umtali Ryder Cup

It is not easy to sum up the life of a man so genial of disposition and generous of heart as Samuel Ryder. It is best left to the minister in his address at Samuel's funeral service. He said, 'they had met to give thanks to God for the life of a good man. Those who knew Samuel Ryder intimately knew how difficult it was to find words with which to speak about him. There were, of course, his great achievements which were widely known. He had the creative imagination and the spark of genius to build up his business, to win fame in the world of sport, to make great contributions to the life of St Albans, and to be prominent in so many forms of social service; but his real greatness lay in the fact that he extended that creative power to everything and to every person whom he met.'

'Because he was so sensitive of soul and felt things intensely, he suffered acutely in the sufferings of others; that anyone should have to bear poverty, ills or pains caused him real sorrow. And yet he was a very happy man, with the happiness of one who could enjoy a good and full life. He took a delight in simple things-'the mirth that hath no bitter stings'; he loved people to be merry and would wish them that day to laugh and rejoice in remembrance of him. He tried to follow the example of his Master, and went about doing good. In that way he found serenity, doing countless acts of kindness with such grace and delicacy that those he helped were never hurt but always blessed by his touch on their lives. There in that church, where he was perfectly at home, his fellow members had sometimes caught glimpses of a truly spiritual mind, of a life of quiet devotion, and realized what his Christian faith and experience really meant to him. When it came to the passing of such a man and such a friend, they were sure that there must be for him somewhere, and in some way, greater enrichment and deeper joy.'

From gardeners and golfers everywhere, thank you Samuel.

144

Bibliography

History of Sale, Norman Swain (1987)

Slater's Directories of Cheshire

Hadfield's Directory of Altrincham (1886)

Merrins Pocket Directory (1886)

St. Albans Almanac

Caseys Directory (1888)

Kellys Directories for Hertfordshire

The Story of St. Albans, Elsie Toms (1975)

Made in St. Albans, Michael Fookes
(1997)

Watchers of a Beacon, Clifford Hodges
(1977)

The Whitcombes – A Golfing Legend,
Peter Fry (1994)

Ryder Cup Heritage, Thomas Anderson-
Davis (1984)

The Ryder Family, Marjorie Claisen (1979)

1993 Ryder Cup Programme

The Ryder Cup, Michael Hobbs (1989)

The Official History of the Ryder Cup,
Michael Williams (1989)

A Confident Century, Stratford-on-Avon
Golf Club 1894-1994, John Gee (1994)

Sale and Stretford Guardian

East Herts and West Essex News

Stratford-upon-Avon Herald

Herts Advertiser

Amateur Gardening

Dorset Evening Echo

The British Golfer

The American Golfer

Golf Illustrated

PGA Journal

Golf Monthly

Golf World

The Times